A Defence of Dogmatism

A Defence of Dogmatism

BY

Harry Blamires

LONDON

S · P · C · K

1965

First published in 1965
by S.P.C.K.
Holy Trinity Church
Marylebone Road
London N.W.1

Printed in Great Britain by
William Clowes and Sons, Limited,
London and Beccles

Contents

Introductory Note

The scheme of this book can be briefly summed up. In chapter 1 I lay before the reader a few instances of the kind of thought and talk which have made the book necessary and desirable. So doing, I touch lightly upon some issues which are more fully examined later on. In chapter 2 I direct attention to the problem of time, because a basic misreading of the nature of time, and of the Christian's position in time, lies at the root of the liberal theologian's misunderstanding and misrepresentation of dogma and dogmatism; and this misreading pushes the liberal into the wrong kind of alliance with secularism. I then make, in chapter 3, (frankly of course and from the dogmatist's point of view) an analysis of some of the differences which distinguish the dogmatist's position from the liberal's, answering especially some of the claims currently made by the liberal for the intellectual position which he adopts towards the dogmatic, and for its alleged contemporary relevance.

Thus, having asserted the overall superiority of the dogmatist's position in terms of contemporary relevance and striking power, as well as in terms of Christian validity, I turn in chapter 4 to show that dogmatism in the religious field is not an isolated survival of an attitude discredited in other fields, but rather an attitude consonant with what experience of human thinking in other important directions presents to us, and likewise consonant especially with the essential nature of the Christian vocation itself. Lastly, in chapter 5, I examine some of the non-theological reasons for being acutely sceptical of the modern scepticism, materialism, and secularism which liberal theology mistakenly tries to accommodate. Thus I illustrate the weakness of the anti-Christian case, and indicate that the rational basis of the Christian dogmatist's position is as sure as it has ever been.

It is fair that I should explain my use of the term *pseudo-theology*. To write pseudo-theology is to use the vocabulary and mechanisms of theological utterance whilst rejecting the presuppositions in favour of the supernatural which would make such usage valid. Any such lapses discovered in this book of mine would rightly be termed "pseudo-theology".

The reader will observe that I have nowhere spoken of "pseudo-theologians". Nor do I wish to imply of any writer into whose work an element of pseudo-theology enters that there will be nothing elsewhere in his work that is valuable and instructive, still less that his theological circle or his literary collaborators are a pack of heretics. Obviously it would be quite improper and misleading to use labels like "the Cambridge theology" simply to describe those elements in the thinking of one or two scholars which one believes to be bad. I trust that my use of the term *pseudo-theology* will be accepted as representing a fair attempt to disentangle from both academic and popular theological thinking certain threads which Christians of many different schools of thought might well like to see discredited.

It scarcely needs saying that I deliberately use the word *dogmatism* in such a way as to rehabilitate an unfashionable concept, and that I am glad to assist in this needful verbal rescue-operation. Conversely I have had to find a word for that contemporary current of theological thinking in which hostility to dogmatism is apparent. I chose the word *liberalism*, as denoting the anti-dogmatic tendency to reconstruct the Christian Faith with an emphasis on the human search rather than on divine revelation. The use of the word *liberalism* over that area of connotation which brings it into collision with the words *dogmatism* and *orthodoxy* is not of course its only possible use (the *Oxford Dictionary of the Christian Church* speaks of the "confusion" surrounding the use of the word), but it is an accredited one. I hope it will not mislead or anger those who are accustomed to give the word *liberalism* (in theology) a more generous range of reference than is brought into play in contexts where orthodoxy and dogmatism are being defended.

1

The Denigration of Dogmatism

Why defend dogmatism? the reader may well ask. Surely the proper need is to defend dogma.

Indeed it might appear that the only logical defence of dogmatism would be that the dogmas referred to are true. It might also appear that the only logical attack on dogmatism would be that the dogmas referred to are false or at least open to question. But we live at a time when the main vocal attack upon dogma in the theological field is not that established doctrines are false—there is a remarkable coyness about declaring anything either true or false—but that they are "irrelevant" or "traditional" (this seems to have become a bad word) or "intellectual" (another bad word). Now it is obviously a waste of time to establish certain doctrines as true for the benefit of people who are not complaining that they are false, but only that they are "irrelevant" or "traditional" or "intellectual", or whatever the latest fashionable pejorative adjective may be. Indeed it might at first sight seem difficult to ascertain exactly what would be the appropriate rational reply to these complaints, for none of the adjectives cited (and one might choose many more from the verbal armoury of the new "liberalism") does in fact commit the user to a judgement that is strictly depreciative.

The truth is that the current liberal attack on dogmatism is not rational but emotive in its expression. If a despairing teacher of a backward class throws up his hands and says, "The trouble is that the Multiplication Tables have become quite irrelevant to the kind of Arithmetic these children are doing", he can scarcely be said to be passing judgement on the Multiplication Tables and recommending their abolition. He is, of course, passing judgement on the current state of the children's educational progress. There may be something for contemporary theological critics to learn from this example. If, on the other hand, our teacher surveys a class of children happily at work with paints and brushes in an Art lesson, and says, "Thank heaven, the Multiplication Tables have become irrelevant to what the children are doing now", he is passing judgement neither on the Multiplication Tables nor on the children's immediate activities. He approves of both, each in its proper sphere.

Some recent spokesmen for liberal theology have tried both to eat their cake and have it. They have loudly proclaimed the *irrelevance* of traditional theological dogmatism in accents so emotively charged as to convey that the doctrines in question can have no significance or value for twentieth-century men and women: but they have carefully avoided (most of them) saying that the doctrines are not true—or even are open to question. In short, they cannot be charged with honestly disputing Christian doctrine, only with furtively discrediting it. Whether the Church has more to fear from the "humanist" who honestly attacks her message from without or from the "theologian" who covertly undermines it from within is a question one dare scarcely press far. But the question faces us.

It is necessary to say this because, amid all the turmoil of the *Honest to God* controversy and kindred controversies, certain smooth voices kept telling us that the only really unhealthy feature of the situation was the violence of the emotions aroused in antagonism to allegedly new and exploratory thinking. But taking into account the foolish utterances which some initiators of controversy committed themselves to, I should be prepared to argue that the violence of the emotions aroused in antagonism was on the contrary the healthiest aspect of a rather unsavoury episode. If implicit attacks on Christian doctrine are made at a sub-rational level on which the weapons of reason are rendered virtually powerless, a special situation is created. No man can argue against a list of contradictions. Yet if it is seen that, threading its way through religious publications which are thus illogical or confused, there runs a vein of emotively powerful but rationally inarticulate depreciation of the Church's status and her message, then the appropriate Christian response may be one of high indignation.

This is not a book within the orbit of any one of the various recent theological controversies; but each of these controversies represented, in my view, a phase in a movement which makes some defence of dogma in principle now highly desirable; some defence, that is, which does not consist in proving dogmatic propositions, but rather in justifying the dogmatic attitude itself, with all the clarity and system that it involves. For there has crept into theological polemics of late a note of irrationalism which could do great damage to our spiritual integrity and our intellectual honesty. We have already mentioned some characteristics of this irrationalism, and many more will be touched on in the course of this book. Basic to this irrationalism is the increasingly advertised notion that there is some incongruity between the Christian religion and the systematic formulation of truths in propositional form. This notion is pressed upon us in utterances which have emotive value rather than rational force. It exerts its influence by a process of denigration that by-passes the difficult paths of lucid argument.

Sometimes the denigration is effected by the use of contrived antitheses which may be valid in one context yet rationally inappropriate in another. For instance, it is often no doubt appropriate to remind ourselves that our Lord was not a professional philosopher but a humble carpenter turned healer. But if you involve yourself in theological argument it may be dishonest and unscrupulous to introduce this reminder just when your

3

argument seems to have landed you in dialectical difficulty. Nevertheless, one has seen reminders of this kind used as escape routes from dialectical defeat. And the device, though irrational, is emotively potent. Your opponent has made a convincing case theologically. You remind him that our Lord was not a scholar or a thinker but a carpenter turned healer. If your opponent gives the appropriate rational reply ("True, but at the moment we are arguing a thesis, not making a table or treating an epileptic"), he can readily be made to appear to have asserted an unworthy and shameful preference for intellectual activity over the simpler and more costly labours that our Lord chose for himself.

It is sad to see the correspondence columns of Christian journals defaced by controversial trickery of this kind. Yet who can deny that this has happened? The controversialist takes the plunge; he is effectively countered and his case lies in ruins. Whereupon he takes up his pen to remind his opponent that the true Christian's faith is centred in a Person—and that Person divine—not in a set of dry intellectual propositions established with mathematical precision on a logical basis. (*Dry*, *intellectual*, *mathematical*, *precision*, *logical*—how potently this vocabulary does its emotive job.) At this point the opponent is virtually made to appear as though, by clearly establishing his polemical victory, he would be casting a slur on something finer and lovelier and more precious than any doctrinal statement, even on the divine figure of our Lord himself. The argument has become one which it would be shame and disgrace to win.

One cannot condemn too severely the recourse to propaganda techniques of this kind in religious controversy. False antitheses between the activities which produce intellectual conclusions, and the suffering, self-giving career of God incarnate, are introduced for the purpose of preventing reason and logic from doing their own proper work in their own proper field. And those who employ the unworthy smothering devices referred to invariably overlook the inner contradiction which their attitude expresses.

4

For even the statement, "The Christian Faith is centred in a Person, not in intellectual propositions", is itself an intellectual proposition. It is therefore subject to all denigrations of intellectual activity and intellectual propositions designed to smother utterances less palatable to those who thus abuse the mechanisms of controversy.

The new pseudo-theology creates in certain circles an atmosphere so emotively charged by what can only be called the slogans of unreason that within it to attempt to make a rational case for a given doctrine is to invite contempt—not because the case is a bad one, but because the attempt itself offends against some undefined code that has now ruled reasoning out of the fashionable theological etiquette. The polemical advantages of clinging to this new code lie in the fact that whether your opponent makes a good case or a bad case is irrelevant to you. You are beyond the reach of reason.

This new code of irrationalism is not of course articulated anywhere. It is kept operative by the repetition of various unexamined slogans and attitudes such as those we have already looked at. It would not be difficult to cite other examples. Take for instance the fashionable talk that "all our traditional concepts (or descriptions) of God must be scrapped". In fact, of course, all concepts, all language, all meaning are handed on in a tradition. Rationality itself is a tradition. A complete rejection of tradition is a rejection of all reason, meaning, and language. Thus the fashionable slogan is meaningless. The word *traditional* does its work for pseudo-theology only by being endowed with an emotively burdened connotation carrying something roughly equivalent to the vague pejorative flavour carried colloquially, in loose usage, by terms like *old-fashioned*, *hidebound*, and *hackneyed*. A fifth-form level of literacy is generally assumed to put one above this kind of thing.

Another fashionable attempt to discredit the rational is represented by such slogans as "There are no glib answers to the questions people are asking the Church" or "We Christians have no easy answers". Now these two statements may be used unexceptionably in certain contexts: but recently words like *glib* and *easy* have been widely utilized for the purpose of discrediting clarity and firmness. In fact, of course, if *glib* is equated with "straight and sharp and clear" (as it appears to be in the minds of "liberals") then there *are* an awful lot of "glib" answers to the questions people are asking the Church. And it is nonsense to pretend that we Christians have not, in a sense, "got" these answers. To assert that we Christians have not got the answers to people's questions, when our Lord has spoken them, martyrs have died to attest their truth, and the saints over so many centuries have been expounding and illustrating them, is to abdicate from our Christian vocation. Let us have no more talk of the Church not having the answers. It has. The answers are our Lord's answers. I do not know what constitutes "glibness", but if we do not claim our Lord and the faith he taught as the sure, clear, straight answers to people's questions, then we have no place among those who choose to represent the Church to the world.

Let it be said firmly that the bogus humility represented by the *We-haven't-got-the-answers* line is as far from true Christian virtue as lust is from love. And indeed it is inconceivable that anyone acquainted with the Gospels should speak as though our Lord himself were incapable of the crisp, the pithy, the devastating come-back. Whatever else our Lord was accused of, he was not charged with preserving a sage and mystical silence whilst the weary and doubtful and dejected and oppressed threw their tragically unanswerable questions at him. Yet in every other religious journal one picks up to-day one reads the amazing sentence: "We must not talk as though we've got all the answers." Why, in God's name, not? What is our Christian duty if not to make plain that in the Christian Faith the gravest doubts and worries of men are richly answered? What do these prevaricators mean? *Have* we not got the answers in their eyes? Is our

6

Lord untrustworthy, the Church founded upon an eternal question-mark, the faith a fog? It will be time enough to put this new slogan on our banners when we have heard a dying martyr proclaim it as the surety of his hope. The scene is worth picturing. The flames gather around the stake, but the martyr's eyes are ablaze only with faith. "I die gladly. I die at peace with God. My last message to you is this: We must not talk as though we've got all the answers!"

The supposed duty of the Christian to take shelter behind a veil of incomprehensibility is an invention of the Devil. The denigration of clarity has no basis in reason or Christianity. Turn to the Gospels and within half an hour you will find a hundred sharp, crisp answers to the questions that press most urgently upon men's minds.

The truth is that pseudo-theology does not like clarity. Hence the depreciation of C. S. Lewis now fashionable in certain circles. We are told, even by *The Times* Obituary, how *The Screwtape Letters* was and is hated. We are not told *by whom*, still less *why*. Indeed, I have never myself been able to elicit from detractors of C. S. Lewis anything more enlightening than that they find him "irritating" or (the bolder ones) "infuriating". This is all very well, but the statements provide no basis for argument. There were people (it is not difficult to categorize them) who no doubt found our Lord's utterances irritating, even infuriating. But whether a written or spoken case is properly judged by being described as either is open to question. "He is irritating" may of course mean no more than "The Christian message, as he represents it, so disturbs my conscience that I prefer not to read him" or "The version of Christian truth his work presents makes me feel uncomfortable as I rest in my familiar and cosy half-truths". On the other hand, "He is irritating" may mean something so totally different as to transform the implicit judgement. It may mean, "This man's misrepresentation of the Christian message is so gross that I am overwhelmed with indignation". Ambiguities

7

covering potential judgements so disparate have no place in honest Christian controversy.

It is high time theological controversialists put their cards on the table. There has been too much sparring from behind masks, too much emotive discrediting of positions which writers have been unwilling to attack openly. Above all, controversy must be lifted above the subrational level at which, of late, even some "academic" theologians have been prepared to operate. To this end the present book is written.

I should like to say, however, that I do not myself accept that there has been a "theological crisis" of the kind pictured by some theological journalists. Still less do I accept that there has been what a writer in *Theology* called "the split between theology and the pastoral ministry". He ought to have said rather "the split between theology and the theologians" or perhaps "the split between *Theology* and the pastoral ministry". But there *has* been a split, and one which makes analysis of the present religious situation in our country complicated. It is difficult to define, but it is based on the fact that there exists among us a vociferous body of religion-discussers who as a group only partially overlap with the religion-practisers. The religion-discussers feed greedily on pseudo-theology; and of course they produce it too. Their apparent influence, in terms of articles in the papers and journals, and of public utterances at meetings and on the air, may be considerable. Their actual influence in terms of minds deeply affected is negligible. They do not appear either to represent or appeal greatly to the solid body of thoughtful Christians whose religious inclinations are manifested in prayer, worship, serious study, and action. (The enormous public that, week by week, year after year, purchases those numberless books of prayer and meditation, those well-worn "classics" of religious instruction which our bookshops feed to them. It is worth remembering that for every single year in which the latest product of off-centre theology stands in piles in the bookshops, there will, thank God, be twenty years in which *Mere Christianity* and *The Screwtape Letters* stand thus available.) Some of the spokesmen of the religion-discussers who make most noise in the world of publicity do of course, by virtue of the sheer amount of time they allot to making this noise, give evidence of personal priorities which thoughtful people note and question.

Moreover, if my experience is any guide, the irrationalism of pseudo-theology is largely a middle-aged phenomenon. The under-thirties, I observe, either practise a religion and believe in it or are uninterested in the subject. Hence the decline of certain societies dedicated to the discussion of religion, which some have much lamented, and over which perhaps we ought to rejoice.

However that may be, the division between religion-discussers and religion-practisers would perhaps justify the atttentions of those who bring statistical and sociological measuring rods to bear on such matters. Certainly the division seems likely to be aggravated if pseudo-theology continues to make use of the smother-talk which is at present being exploited for the purpose of denigrating faithfulness in worship and prayer. One has read, for instance, the phrase "the traditionally pious" used sneeringly of the faithful in worship, used in a context which would make it appear that there are now "Christian" mentalities to whom both tradition and piety are offensive. One has also heard, for instance, the word "pharisaical" used as though, in certain circles, it were automatically accepted as the appropriate term to characterize a person regular in public worship and plainly given to an ordered life within the Church's discipline, who happened to be unwilling to admit that his beliefs were anyway weakened or affected by the latest utterance from a liberal theologian publicly advertising some new stage in his loss of faith. It is surely an evil perversion of language to apply the word "pharisaical" to the Christian whose religious faith and practice are quietly persisted in, without the flicker of an eyelid, while listener-research registers the rise and fall of pop-clerics peddling heresy. Only in an unhealthy intellectual atmosphere could verbal perversions of this kind pass muster for enlightened thinking. Never did the Church stand more in need of the sharp disinfectant that dogmatism provides.

2

The Tyranny of Time

The modern mind is bemused by a misreading of the nature of time. Some years ago I wrote a book (*The Faith and Modern Error*) in which an attempt was made to exemplify some of the prevailing errors derivative from the dominant false philosophy of our age, its Naturalism, that is, its acceptance of the natural order as the only reality, the only source of meaning, purpose, and value. I pin-pointed certain current manifestations of Individualism and Materialism—in their neat form, as stock themes of our secular thinking, and in their diluted form, as infecting thought within the Church itself. Pursuing the diagnosis of modern error further, I would now add the false notion of time to the list of seminal illusions which do widespread damage to our culture generally and to our religious thinking in particular.

Few Christians would quarrel with the statement that an irrational veneration for time corrupts our secular culture. Secularism is, by definition, time-locked. And since I have been misunderstood in the past, may I make plain that I use the words *secular* and *secularism* strictly. The sphere of the secular is a sphere untouched by religion. In so far as it is penetrated by the religious, the secular to that extent ceases to be purely secular. (Thus, unlike the Anglican Communion, the domain of the secular has this characteristic, that its vocation is to disappear.)

Secularism is time-locked in that it accepts time as a determinative dimension. It makes no attempt to *overlook* the temporal. It does not take eternity seriously into account. If it did, it would cease to be secularism. It follows that secularism, wherever it is self-confident, will believe in progress. As it has no eternity to trust in (and it regards its past as dead), it must necessarily look to the future for the fulfilment of its hopes and aspirations. In so far as the secular mind looks out upon an imperfect society, recognizing its deficiencies, it must either despair or believe that the deficiencies can and will be corrected in the future. The purpose, therefore, of self-confident secularism is keyed to an all-important temporal future.

The breakdown of secular self-confidence is invariably represented by a collapse of belief in progress. This breakdown may or may not be accompanied by recourse to the religious, but it is necessarily attended, wherever it is articulate, by a probing reassessment of the significance of time. It is no accident that some of the profoundest works of imaginative literature that our century has produced reveal what can only be called an obsession with the problem of time. Proust's *A la Recherche du Temps Perdu*, Joyce's *Ulysses*, Eliot's *The Waste Land* and *Four Quartets* provide crucial testimony here, and this chapter will have to refer again to the cultural state of mind which such literature reflects. At a less profound level, but in perhaps sharper focus, books like Aldous Huxley's *Brave New World* and George Orwell's *1984* present Time the great Healer as finally dethroned, and Time the Despoiler in control.

Of course ours is not the first age in which imaginative writers have tussled with the problem of time. Indeed, in all ages, sensitive artists have identified the ravages of time as one of the human spirit's most testing burdens. No doubt it is in moments at which the values of their civilization have seemed least estimable that great writers have probed most searchingly into the problem of time, and a work which would deserve close analysis by anyone anxious to explore this issue further is Shakespeare's *Troilus and Cressida*. Thus, though twentieth-century writers are not the first to worry about time (one might argue that as Eliot's

Four Quartets centre on the problem of time, so Keats's *Odes* centre on the same subject), nevertheless the nearly simultaneous and emphatic concern of several very great writers with this issue, and at a profound level, is notable.

We have said that the breakdown of secular self-confidence will be represented by a collapse of belief in progress: and belief in progress is trust in the future as being likely to provide the answers to the problems and needs of the present. If this is a true definition of belief in progress and of what secular self-confidence involves, it follows that there is an inverse relationship between secular self-confidence and religious insight such as Christianity provides. Christianity is not time-locked. Its spiritual and moral disciplines are geared to the process of deflecting us from focusing our hopes and desires too firmly on a temporal future. Our hearts and wills have to be weaned from reliance upon tomorrow or next month or next year.

For the Christian, time, *as understood by the secularist*, is a limiting, not a liberating dimension. (At this point the distinctions I wish to make almost tempt me to use the phrases *secular time* and *Christian time*, but I find them semantically offensive and theologically dangerous.) The passage of time, as secularly conceived, cuts man off from the past irrevocably, whereas the Christian is forever involved in activities like prayer and worship in which he is at one with his fellows of centuries back.

It seems to the present writer that the health and soundness of current theological and religious trends can perhaps best be gauged by measuring how far, at base, these trends transcend, or merely reflect, buoyant secularism's unquestioning confidence in the temporal; how far they unconsciously give precedence to an unexamined trust in progress. It will surely be agreed that developing Christian awareness, at whatever cultural level, will make a man increasingly dissatisfied with secularism's blinkered veneration for time, increasingly critical of secularism's wild trust in the future as the bountiful provider of answers, fulfilments, solutions, realizations (of questions, hopes, problems, dreams).

If this reasoning is sound, one is driven to the conclusion, hard and sweeping though it may appear, that much in recent theological thinking has been marred by the persistence in ostensibly Christian writing of a secularist estimate of the significance of time. Some of the more extravagant propositions of Bishop Robinson and of so-called "Cambridge" theology are sub-Christian in that they give voice to an excessive secularist confidence in the temporal future as the purveyor of answers and solutions. Thus I would argue that a fundamental philosophical error behind the vagaries of *Honest to God* and *Soundings* is failure to consider adequately the relationship between the temporal and the eternal. The fundamental theological error is probably failure to reckon with the doctrine of the Ascension.

Nowhere are these failures more apparent than in Dr Vidler's Introduction to *Soundings*.[1]

> The Authors of this volume of essays cannot persuade themselves that *the time is ripe* for major works of theological construction. *It is time for ploughing, not reaping;* or, to use the metaphor we have chosen for our title, *it is time for making soundings, not charts or maps.* If this be so, we do not have to apologize for *our inability to do what we hope will be possible in a future generation.* We can best serve the cause of truth and of the Church by candidly confessing where our perplexities lie, and not *by making claims which,* so far as we can see, *theologians are not at present in a position to justify.*

And later—

> Our task is to try to see what the questions are that we ought to be facing in the nineteen-sixties. *It goes without saying that they are different from what they were in the eighteen-sixties.* . . . We do not wish to evade the assessment of our work by our contemporaries—we shall welcome it; but *we believe we are*

[1] *Soundings, Essays concerning Christian Understanding.* C.U.P.

handling questions that are not likely to receive definitive answers for a long time to come. (My italics.)

I do not think it would be unjust to this Introduction to claim that many of its phrases hint at an unexamined presupposition in favour of the doctrine of progress as it was widely held a hundred years ago. The notion that "important" theological questions remain to be explored patiently for coming decades and even centuries while intellectual conviction is held in a state of prolonged suspense is not christianly tenable. Of course, if theologians reply that by "important" they do not mean important (that is, of crucial significance to living Christians, of direct relevance to the salvation of souls), well and good. If they mean that *minor* or *trivial* theological questions remain to be answered, let them say so, and we will agree with them.

It would be a formidable task to dig out and expose all the various secularist prejudices which recent theological vagaries exemplify. Here it must suffice to uncover one or two which are strongly relevant to our main theme. In the Introduction to *Soundings* the concealed presupposition in favour of a secularist doctrine of progress is matched by a concealed secularist assumption that the human situation generally offers men and women the kind of ease, plenty, and comfort which encourage calm speculation, reflective discussion, and the steady ripening of understanding. The metaphor of the ship which gives the volume its title is highly significant here. It sounds a pretty well-equipped vessel. The sea is apparently calm. There is leisure and time to take patient soundings without the pressure of particular urgency.

Now I do not complain only that this is not the human situation as the Christian understands it, though the point must be made. The Christian imagery of the ages has presented us with a picture of our course through life in very different terms. If we are afloat, it is upon a stormy sea. The physical conditions give us time and respite to cry for mercy, but little more. The notion that we have years of welfare-cushioned calm ahead of us in which to measure the deep ways of God reflects a dangerous complacency. (The "temper" both of Dr Robinson's and Dr Vidler's forward-looking utterances is as clearly the product of long years of peace and affluence as the "temper" of *The Screwtape Letters* is the product of war.) But more remarkably the notion springs from precisely the kind of thinking from which the writers are pretending to escape. That is to say, it is culturally a hundred years out of date. It establishes in the theological field a notion of the human situation which disappeared from the field of serious culture some fifty years ago. Some at least of the contributors to *Soundings* ought to read a little literature as a change from watching films of dubious artistic value. Certain it is that no one familiarly acquainted with the work of Kafka, Proust, Joyce, Eliot, Camus, Beckett, and their peers, could imagine that the modern mind, at the cultural level, thinks of the human situation as offering the kind of progress, security, and confidence tacitly presupposed by the Introduction to *Soundings*. Life is not a steady pilgrimage in the eyes of the sensitive modern European. Life is an emergency. It is perhaps an absurdity. It is perhaps desperate, perhaps farcical, perhaps worthless, but it is not, certainly not, a calm voyage on which soundings can patiently be taken. And if it is argued that scholarship must always make the presupposition in favour of leisured calm and security, then it must be replied that, in that sense, scholarship will always be out of touch with living reality. The truth is that theology, like imaginative literature, has to be deeper and more sensitive than mere "scholarship"—for the very reason that the writers of *Soundings* would themselves surely appreciate; that is to say, to preserve it from remoteness and unreality.

In the world of culture as represented by imaginative literature, the nineteenth-century picture of life in terms of progress, increasing understanding, increasing mastery, patient discovery, has been violently displaced. Instead of it, twentieth-century writers present us with a picture of life in terms of crisis, emergency, absurdity, and horror. This change in itself represents a reassessment of the terrestrial and the finite which obviously invites a reassertion of the religious. In some cases in the literary field—in the poetry of T. S. Eliot and David Jones, for instance —that reassertion has been made with peculiar relevance and assurance, also with a notable theological rigidity, and has been received with the maximum respect and understanding by cultured unbelievers generally.

But now, when the cultural situation, as represented by the state of imaginative literature, calls firmly for a religious judgement upon the secular appropriate to the intellectual abdication of secularist optimism, we have the absurd spectacle of eminent theologians rushing headlong backwards to buttress the already fallen ramparts of nineteenth-century Naturalism. The spectacle is both comic and tragic. Consider some of the great representative voices of Victorian England—say Dickens, Tennyson, and Browning. It would not be unjust to claim that in each of these three writers the religious is exploited as an appendage to optimistic secularism. The claim does not impugn the sincerity of any of these writers: it merely notes the limitations of their religious understanding on the one hand, and of their religious commitment on the other, at a time when these limitations were perhaps less under pressure than they would be now. These writers use the religious primarily to reinforce the values and virtues of humane secularism, to give an added dimension to their temporal confidence. By contrast the work of T. S. Eliot asserts the religious in its own right as automatically and inevitably bringing a judgement upon the secular. The cultural revolution which this development represents has been overlooked in theology by the very scholars who pride themselves on their progressiveness. Despite superficial appearances, there is a deep level at which the Introduction to *Soundings*, like *Honest to God*, is simply old-fashioned. In the chronology of culture the two are roughly contemporaneous with Tennyson's *In Memoriam*. (The specific resemblances between *Honest to God* and *In Memoriam* would provide material for an interesting essay.)

In touching upon this controversy it is necessary to anticipate a point that will be more fully developed in chapter 3, and to defend oneself in advance against the fallacious argument by which exponents of *we-shall-know-later-on* theology sometimes attack their more "dogmatic" opponents. It is claimed that the theology of indefinitely extended progress towards truth represents humility, in that it rejects the "presumptuous" claim of dogmatists to know all the answers already. This fallacious argument has done great damage, and it is important to reveal its perversity. In fact it exactly reverses the true picture. The theology of indefinitely extended progress towards truth is itself presumptuous because it is based on the assumption that men are going to learn more about God in this life than in fact they are capable of learning. The theology of dogmatism accepts that men are not going to know, intellectually, any more about God in this life than has already been revealed to them; that they will have to make the best of what they have got. In short the dogmatists accept the limitations of the human intellect before the mystery and profundity of Godhead. They recognize that God has mercifully broken through to man fully and overtly at the physical level in the familiar categories of human existence once and once only. From that breaking-through, that revelation, and its consequences, has been derived a distinct but limited intellectual knowledge of the eternal appropriate to human needs and human capacities. It has been given. The dogmatist rejects as presumptuous the notion that men of their own skill and search can significantly extend the scope of that knowledge. The dogmatist's humbler estimate of the range and potentiality of human understanding leads him to cling firmly to what God has given man in revelation. It is not that he believes man's present formulation of this knowledge to be either perfect or adequate. He accepts its inadequacy—but it is an inadequacy that can be measured only against the adequacy of the eternal. The inadequacy, we may say, is part of the game. It is a built-in feature of the human situation. The *we-shall-know-later-on* theologian presupposes that the human understanding will in time (yes, *in time*) attain more adequate knowledge of God. The dogmatist has no such confidence in man's powers. Nor has he confidence that the course of life is ever likely to be such as profoundly to change man's capacities for penetrating the infinite from within the boundaries of time.

Common sense corroborates the dogmatist's refusal to play too glibly the intellectual game in relation to the things of God. Does the Cambridge theologian of the nineteen-sixties understand the nature of God better than, say, John Donne understood it? If he does, we are anxious to share this understanding, and we eagerly await the moment when he will make it public. If he does not, then what reason has he for expecting the theologian of the twenty-sixties, or for that matter of the twenty-four-sixties, to understand the nature of God better than we do to-day?

The vagaries of the new theological liberalism have been shown by various genuine theological scholars to be neither new nor revolutionary. They have been shown to re-hash heresies discredited earlier in Christian history. But a movement such as they represent might be theologically old-fashioned and disreputable and yet be in tune with vital movements of current secular thought. My own concern here is to assert that in fact the new pseudo-theology is as much out of key with the intelligent contemporary cultural drift as it is with true theological scholarship.

I do not pretend that this is a subject on which one can speak with scientific decisiveness. The larger movements of thought in our culture become apparent only to hindsight and can be clearly defined only by the historian. Nevertheless, we need not for that reason deny ourselves the exercise of trying to discern the present as it will look to the future. To do this penetratingly in the field of literature might produce some salutary shocks. For instance it could be argued that the future literary scholar, drawing comparisons between the Victorian Age and our own age, might have ample reason to reverse many of the judgements generally accepted in popular thinking to-day.

To illustrate this point, let us picture a scholar a century hence looking back, first on the work of Tennyson, Arnold, Browning, Swinburne, Dickens, George Eliot, Thackeray, Trollope, and Meredith; then on the work of Eliot, Pound, Auden, David Jones, Yeats, Joyce, Lawrence, Greene, and Beckett. Might he not arrive at some such judgement as the following:

"The Victorian Age was one of complacency. In its literature the dimension of the spiritual was largely unexplored and the truly religious was overlaid by a sentimental religiosity which some writers rejected for its shallowness and others accepted as an ornament to trick out their humanitarianism and their idealism. By contrast, the first half of the twentieth century, to judge from its literature, was an age of sharpened religious consciousness. Among imaginative writers the numerical relationship between Christians and non-Christians probably changed little from the one century to the other. But in the twentieth century dominant imaginative writers, believers and unbelievers alike, subjected contemporary civilization and current values to a ruthless scrutiny which was rooted in an acute religious sensitivity to the spiritual nature of man and to the mystery of being. On the evidence of its imaginative literature, the early twentieth century was blessed with a religious consciousness more widely awake than it had been at any time since the seventeenth century."

It would not perhaps be proper (though it would be polemically palatable) to put into the mouth of our hypothetical future scholar the appropriate footnote to describe the efforts of those theologians of the nineteen-sixties who imagined that the cultural climate was ripe for a readjustment of the religious demand so as to accommodate an already defunct secular self-confidence. The case I would press does not need to be bolstered by hypothesis. It is simply this. If our greatest literature truly represents the temper of current thinking at the cultural level, then our new theologians are better fitted for converse with our great-grand-fathers than for converse with the alert young minds of to-day who have been nourished on the cultural inheritance of their own age.

Of course we must not claim that the assumptions of those who write or respond to the best imaginative literature are likely to express the quantitatively dominant spirit of the age. Our *mass* culture has a materialistic bias which educated men of very different beliefs alike reject and condemn. But there are, deeply embedded in our élite cultural life to-day, veins of religious awareness and of secular despair to which the needle of theology must penetrate. That is where an injection of faith can be effective.

The failure of the "new theology" to answer any of the hungers of our age is inevitable. (Indeed it would be tragic were the case otherwise—were there a secularist intelligentsia so be-mused by finite aims and terrestrial satisfactions that they grasped with both hands at a secularized theology to nourish their secular buoyancy.) This is partly because what I have called the religious awareness revealed in much modern literature has, even though it sometimes assumes a sceptical front, an intellec-tual, moral, and spiritual depth that the "new theology" lacks. And it is partly because the "new theology", by virtue of its built-in veneration for the future, and its consequent naïve pre-supposition in favour of the doctrine of progress, would try to lead the mind of the modern intellectual back into a servitude to the temporal from which crucial cultural developments have some decades ago liberated him.

An important psychological factor which has affected recent theological controversy is the thirst for revolution. Christian orthodoxy is always revolutionary in that it challenges the purely temporal criteria of secular society by reference to the eternal. The revolutionary demands of Christian orthodoxy are far-reaching in that they call the individual to a series of virtual contradictions of the familiar established ethics of time-locked pragmatism and hedonism which motivate our thinking in personal and public life. The costliness of the inescapable Christian dissidence, in terms of misunderstanding by others, nervous tension, sacrifice of popularity and "togetherness", may be severe (though no doubt the "contrasuggestive" personality in a sense enjoys paying such a price). It is of course easier and more attractive to align oneself with the world's wisdom and its values than to question them. Thus a peculiar temptation faces the Christian. He is lured to satisfy the revolutionary hunger which the faith inevitably implants in him by aligning himself with some form of secular radicalism, and investing the radical principles with a false Christian garb on the grounds that those principles (like the Church) challenge the secular establishment. The secular Establishment is (quite properly *up to a point*) identified with "the World". The radical secular programme is (quite *improperly*, for the most part) identified with Christianity.

The next step in this devious sequence is to identify institutional aspects of Christianity with the secular Establishment on the deceptive (but superficially plausible and emotively powerful) grounds that both represent the fixed, the conservative, the unchanging. The net result of this process is the hardly disentangleable jumble of heresies, superstitions, half-truths, and errors with genuine insights, idealisms, reforming zeal, and honest indignation, which alternately entertains and saddens readers of "with-it" theological journalists and writers. Thus, in place of the true Christian message, calling to penitence and self-surrender, the true Christian voice calling to rejection of the world's values and criteria, we hear an incoherent sub-Christian scream, illogically inviting us to throw over Catholic doctrine and established ecclesiastical machinery in the name of a code of progress towards greater independence and freedom which is wholly secular in its basis and orientation.

Other writers have exemplified the irrationality and incoherence of recent pseudo-theology so finely and lucidly that there is no cause to continue the work of demolition here. I would only wish to pick out some aspects of recent controversy which bear upon my central theme. In particular I would stress that pseudo-theology is always seeking to satisfy the revolutionary need implanted by the faith and left hungry by refusal to feed on the austere and costly claims of orthodoxy. One device for achieving this spurious satisfaction is to confuse the Christian ethic with the hedonistic drift towards free-thinking and free-love, and with the latest clap-trap from the popular psychology front. Progress down this particular vicious whirlpool is made with remarkable ease. Note how it happens. Christianity demands the revolutionary posture *vis-à-vis* the World: but the victim of pseudo-theology has abandoned the supernatural premises which would give the revolutionary posture its purpose and its justification. Hungry for the revolutionary posture, the victim of pseudo-theology seizes upon some cause which, though basically this-worldly in its nature, yet carries with it the emotive current of a challenge to the established order in the name of individualism. A little bit of verbal sleight of hand with words like *freedom* and *love* and *person* is practised, and the New Morality is born.

There is another trick by which a false revolutionary status is purchased for pseudo-theology. This trick is peculiarly characteristic of thinking that is incurably secular, especially in respect of its servitude to time. The trick consists in positing a Christianity that is in perpetual revolution against itself—a Christianity for ever changing and growing by the discovery and correction of past error.

Difficult as it may be to make the point in such a way that the secularized mind can grasp it, one must state that this assumption represents a grievous error. It tries to give a purely temporal character to that which is eternal. The changelessness of the Christian Faith is a supra-temporal changelessness. It has little connection with that persistence of certain forms and attitudes through long stretches of time which brings the word "conservative" into play. The doctrine of the Trinity is changeless, not in the sense that it has stood the test of time, but in the sense that it is not subject to the test of time. Thus the equations made, in political and social thinking, between the established and the defunct or moribund, between the new and the vital, are totally inapplicable to the field of Christian doctrine, and largely so to the field of Christian action. The changelessness of Christian truth and Christian practice manifests neither a natural toughness against the ravages of time nor an inert moribundity before the vital flow of time. Rather it manifests a supernatural basis that confers superiority to the effects of the temporal process.

We have said that Christianity's spiritual and moral disciplines deflect us from focusing our hopes and desires too firmly on a temporal future. Note the conflict here. For the secularist the past is dead and all hope is centred in the future. For the Christian the past is alive and hope must be centred, not in the future, but in God's eternity. Secularism is enslaved to the future both morally and intellectually. The Christian is called to escape both of these servitudes. Moral servitude is shown when human desire and appetite fix their grasp upon the future in the possessive quest for satisfaction. Intellectual servitude is shown when the brain fixes its grasp upon the future in the possessive quest for meaning. If this is so, then the pseudo-theology of the nineteen-sixties is related at a deep level to the avaricious impulses that permeate social life.

The principle that we must accept the present as sufficient to itself has both intellectual and moral implications. It is in the present that the eternal can be known; it is in the present that the past can be recovered; it is in the present that the future can be accepted—without hunger, without the outstretched hand clutching at satisfactions temporally withheld, at meaning temporally unconfirmed. We must not be impatient with the present. We must be suspicious of the contemporary, but never impatient with the present. Dissatisfaction with the limitations of the present in relation to idealized future or idealized past is not an indulgence open to the Christian. Above all, the assumption that one must look to the future for the meaning which will answer current intellectual hunger is one that cuts across the grain of Christianly directed thinking. It is a false basis for the construction of mental attitudes, just as the assumption that the future will answer to-day's desires is an unsound basis for the adoption of emotional attitudes.

To take up one's stance in the present in a posture that is insecure or tentative by reference to a hypothetical future which will provide the assurance and certainty lacking to-day is not a Christian option, because it tries to give to the temporal future a status that properly belongs to the eternal. To look to the future to provide meaning where now is meaninglessness, assurance where now is doubt, wisdom where now is darkness, coherence where now is disorder—this is to by-pass the eternal and to commit oneself to idolatry before the temporal process. It is to commit in the intellectual sphere the error which is parallel to the sin of avarice in the moral sphere. It is to embrace with the intellect a philosophy of worldliness all the more dangerous because the commitment is unrecognized.

Neither as stretching out before individual man in his personal life, nor as stretching forward before a generation in the history yet to be, does the future contain answers, solutions, coherences, and discoveries to which we must reach and yearn for illumination, guidance, and certainty. Meaning, direction, and assurance are on offer, not in a temporal future, as the Marxist and the materialist and pseudo-theology teach, but in God's eternity, as our Lord taught. They are on offer in just such balance and quantity, clarity and "comfort", as is good for us to sense and savour in the judgement of Divine Providence. The proper relationship of the temporal to the eternal is just such a relationship of dependence as that.

The moral aspect of our creatureliness before the Creator is that we are not in a position to take over the direction of his universe in our own unguided wilfulness. The intellectual aspect of our creatureliness before the Creator is that we are not going to get *in time* the answers which God's eternity exists to provide, the assurance which comes only from rootedness in that eternity. The moral aspect of our childlikeness before the Father is that we are not by status or nature independent enough to be thrown out of the family to start our own little rival families in competitive universes. The intellectual aspect of our childlikeness before the Father is that we are not going to be allowed to add fact to fact, discovery to discovery, until we have become as gods within the framework of time.

The idolatry of the temporal process implicit in much recent theological thinking should now be evident. It is of course no accident that the pseudo-theology of men who accept an intellectual servitude to time should be accompanied by unease before the traditional formulations of the eternal/temporal relationship. The creatureliness of the human creature, the childhood status of the human creature, and the Fatherhood of God are brought into question, and fashionable talk about man growing up and becoming adult adds to that total misreading of the temporal situation which disfigures our age's thinking. A key error threading its furtive way through recent pseudo-theology is that "time will tell".[1] It will not. Eternity will tell.

The intellectual position of John Robinson (A.D. 2137–2200)

---

[1] *Honest to God*, Introduction. "The one thing of which I am fairly sure is that, in retrospect, it will be seen to have erred in not being nearly radical enough."

vis-à-vis eternity will be exactly the same as the position of his twentieth-century ancestor. So far as the great choices of faith or doubt, hope or despair, are concerned, he will have no intellectual advantages over his great-great-great-great-grandfather. The supernatural challenge presented to him by the Gospel will be no less disturbing to his natural appetites, no less formidable to his intellect, for the passage of time from now. He will be unwise, in A.D. 2180, to rest in uncertainty before the Christian demand in the hope that A.D. 2190 will provide the answers to his questions. He will be unwise, in A.D. 2190, to write a book challenging the traditional, orthodox formulations of the Christian Faith on the grounds that A.D. 2240 will surely see the emergence of a new breed of theologians at last equipped to clear away the lumber of the centuries from the Christian mind. He will be foolish indeed to committ himself, in A.D. 2190, in public utterance to the view that whatever he says then about the misguidedness of the great doctors and fathers will later "in retrospect" from the twenty-third century, seem "not nearly radical enough".

How can we save the John Robinsons of the twenty-second and twenty-third centuries from error? How can we forestall that tyranny of time over the minds and hearts of men by virtue of which the future dangles its false allurements to confuse the brain and trouble the passions? We cannot. A built-in condition of the human situation is that life should be thus and thus. It will never be easy to look to eternity for satisfaction, to eternity for meaning. It will always be more attractive superficially to look to the future for both; more attractive to set one's heart on the future, one's mind on the future, than to focus both on things above. But there can be no mistake about our Lord's instructions in this matter.

The effects of recent attempts to obliterate the supra-temporal dimension from our mental life will perhaps some day be systematically tabulated by historians curious about the aberrations of our day. One effect is the replacement of dogma by opinion, and of authoritative teaching by perpetually self-renewing discussion. Another effect—which markedly characterizes our civilization—is the shift from concentration upon God and his omnipotence as the creative principle and source of being at the supernatural level, to concentration on woman and her sexuality as the creative principle and source of being at the natural level. The narrowing of the eternal to the temporal perspective inevitably effects this shift, and it is thus logically to be expected that a pseudo-theology blinkered by temporality should be obsessed by sex. It is likewise to be expected that a civilization engaged in tearing man from his roots in the supernatural should substitute the mystique, the rituals, and the doctrines of sexuality for those of the Christian Faith. That this transference of human interest has taken place will readily be acknowledged by anyone who can compare the art, literature, buildings, and habits of the medieval city with those of the modern city. (I am not suggesting that there is necessarily more sexual activity, more natural—or even un-natural—sexual intercourse in the twentieth century than there was in the Middle Ages; only that sexuality to-day is much more dwelt upon, talked of, and celebrated.)

Obliteration of the supernatural dimension from our thinking inevitably shifts human attention from the vessels of the new birth—font, and chalice, and Virgin's womb—to the vessel of the old birth, the womb of woman taken and impregnated. It is no mere coincidence that the same decade should have seen the rise of a pseudo-theology heavily this-worldly in its dominant interests and the full flowering of a popular fiction which is vagina-centred in its dominant interests. Coition replaces Communion as the most venerated act of daily life. The meeting of the eternal and the temporal in the Church's sacred mystery is replaced by the mingling of balanced temporalities in the sexual act. That an ecclesiastic should pronounce the sex act, even outside marriage, as a valid act of communion analogous to the Church's rite is interesting in this connection.

The Christian's proper awareness of the present holds it over against eternity. It is the unfailing sense of the present's relationship to eternity that gives Christian thinking and living its essential character of daring, depth, assurance, and clarity. This is true of experience over a wide area. T. S. Eliot has reminded us that Annunciation and Incarnation, archetypally considered and personally repeated in the lives of Christians, represent points of intersection of the timeless with time. So does the moment of Consecration in the Eucharist; so too does the mystic's experience of disciplined peace or sudden illumination. Every sacrament brings a moment of such intersection; every prayer, every turning to God, is a momentary escape from the tyranny of time. It follows that the more surely the Christian lives in prayer and contemplation, in sacrament and discipline, the more fully he will sense the present as deriving its meaning, its richness, its validity, from the eternal; and the less will he be able to sympathize with an outlook that casts forward into the future for that light and significance which only the eternal can give and only the present can now hold.

The present has depth by virtue of its openness to the eternal; the present has meaning by virtue of its transparency to the eternal. Neither depth nor meaning can be given to the present as a moving moment hurrying through linear time to the future. If we accept the model of linear time, then the future is unreachable and the past forever lost. But the Christian is committed to a view of time less fettering than that. The present is open and transparent to an eternity in which the past still lives and the future is already held. In our Lord past and present and future are gathered together. By virtue of the fact that our present is open to eternity, the past is forever recovered and relived.

The Christian finds no difficulty in believing that St Peter, St Paul, St Augustine, St Francis, and St Thomas Aquinas are alive now in Christ: but he seems to be losing sight of many of the far-reaching implications of this truth. He accepts it for liturgical purposes as he studies the calendar of the Church's year, but he tends to forget its relevance to his religious thinking generally. And yet, in times of doubt and distrust especially, there is no more comforting and reassuring doctrine in the Christian's armour of rationality than this.

The armour is much needed at this present moment. The tyranny of time has operated, outside the Church and within it, to produce a false and dangerous sense of our togetherness with our contemporaries only and our separateness from those who have lived in the past. We suffer from a grossly exaggerated notion of the significance of sheer contemporaneousness. And we suffer from a correspondingly inflated estimate of the isolation of the present from the past. There is no justification, either in Christianity or reason, for the highly pressurized notion of our need at all costs to be *with* those who are living on this earth at the same time as ourselves. On the contrary there is every justification of truth and reason for cultivating the awareness of our unbreakable links with fellow-Christians in the past. And not only must we nourish our sense of our links with fellow-Christians in the past; we must heed our undoubted responsibilities towards them, responsibilities in many cases intensified by sufferings and martyrdoms endured in our Lord's Name in ages harsher physically to the Christian than our own.

The proximity of mere contemporaneousness ought surely not to weigh too heavily with the man who believes that in eternity past and present are one and that in Christ Christians of all ages are alive together. The proximity of mere contemporaneousness is perhaps trivial compared to the proximity of congeniality, that is, the proximity of those whose mutually shared sympathies and insights unite them across the centuries. Proximity in time is in itself surely of no more significance than proximity in space. The fact that one shares with another the same lift, or the same railway compartment, day after day, year after year, in itself provides no rational basis for mutual sympathy and intellectual commerce comparable to that provided by the fact that one, shall we say, reads the same books or has the same kind of job as another person whom one rarely encounters—locally. The fact that one shares with another the same decade likewise in itself provides no rational basis for mutual sympathy and intellectual commerce comparable to that provided by deeply shared convictions and interests that unite people across the centuries.

It is important to remember this at a time when the morale of the Church is being shaken by shallow heresies whose drawing power is alleged to reside in their modernity. There is no reason or virtue in being attuned to any notion or practice simply on the grounds that it is currently fashionable. There is no special demand upon us to agree with a person simply because he is alive. Indeed there may well be a much more cogent demand upon us to agree with a person precisely because he is dead—in that he died for the belief we are being asked to preserve. At a time when Catholic orthodoxy is being assailed by peripheral aberrations whose main platform is that they are truly contemporary, it is wise to remind ourselves that this platform is a shaky one. That a group of vocal clergy who misunderstand the Christian Faith in the doctrinal or the moral field, or in both, should advertise themselves by drawing attention to the fact that these are the nineteen-sixties and that they and we are alive together at this juncture, is a matter of clinical interest only. The categories of truth and falsehood, reason and unreason, remain unaffected by the accident of contemporaneousness. We must never look at contemporary heresy simply in its contemporary context. We must see it against the background of the massive, ageless Christian orthodoxy which is rooted in what is timeless.

In short, it would be foolish for the Christian to worry because he felt that his dearest Christian convictions cut him off from the present Bishop of X, Dean of Y, or Chaplain of Z. But he would have grave cause for worry if he suddenly discovered that one of his earnestly held "Christian" convictions cut him off from

St Augustine, St Francis, or St Theresa. It is difficult to persuade those who regard the Church as a purely temporal institution in perpetual revolution against itself that the arguments they tend to use in pressing their claims themselves constitute an invalidation of those claims. But such is the case. For to urge that we should shake off the past is in fact to urge that we should cease to be Christians. Christians cannot shake off the past. It is alive unto God in Jesus Christ our Lord.

Those Christians who enjoy some kind of intellectual or cultural life will of course be the quickest to find the assertions of pseudo-theology on this topic repellent. No man is happy to learn one morning from the front page of a newspaper or from the latest paperback that his life-long friendship and understanding through the printed word with John Donne or Jeremy Taylor, George Herbert or John Bunyan, has been based on a misunderstanding. He will naturally resent the claim that these were nice gentlemen after their fashion and indeed tolerably instructed for their day, but had the misfortune to live too soon to be acquainted with the true nature of God as recently stumbled upon by a German philosopher and the proper function of religion as shortly to be explained by an English suffragan bishop.

Let us preserve our sense of humour. God knows, we are going to need it before the pseudo-theology of the sixties has fully run its course. It is of course no mere sentimentality, no mere anachronism on our part, no legalism or obscurantism, not even pharisaism or hardness of heart, which urges us to be *with* the great and the less great Christians of the past, even if it means being against a handful of our noisier contemporaries. Rather it is an impulse deeply rooted in Christian instinct and reason. If X is a heretic, bent on weakening the fabric of Christian doctrine, then the fact that he is alive to-day gives his views no greater weight than they had at their last airing, whether it was one or two or fourteen centuries ago. Contemporary heresy has of course a proper claim on our attention in so far as it is capable of misleading our fellows and our children. But that attention will not be properly rendered more sympathetic by the fact that the heresy seems to have immediate potentiality for damaging souls. Rather the attention will be properly rendered more alertly critical and sharp.

We have reason to speculate about what is our moral duty in cases of this kind. Study of theological controversy over the last year or two suggests that Christians sound in faith and doctrine have tended to indulge the intellectual aberrations of pseudo-theology unwarrantably. The motives no doubt have been worthy, the intentions sincere. Thus, instructed theologians have leaned over backwards, in commenting upon the utterances of pseudo-theology, in the effort to preserve the pretence that X's views are worth weighing, should be given attention, must be further pondered, and so on. This, in reference often to arguments so deficient in logic and understanding that in healthy academic institutions students would be justly rebuked by their tutors for presenting them on paper. If, in the name of tolerance and charity, we treat too tenderly utterances which show grave deficiencies of understanding, logic, and sheer literacy, we risk doing a grave disservice to the Christian cause. Not only do we betray criteria and standards whose support we badly need in the struggle against paganism, we also weaken the authority of truth, wisdom, and reason over against falsehood, foolishness, and irrationality. No doubt we are morally justified in taking the maximum care not to humiliate a man of some position in the ecclesiastical or academic world by ruthlessly analysing the defects of understanding which mar his published work, but we have to be correspondingly careful of those souls likely to be misled by his own confusion and ignorance. The complexity of the moral dilemma that has faced many Churchmen in this respect has not been the least of our worries during the last few years. It is well enough for us who know that academic position —even in the ancient universities—is no guarantee of capacity to reason or to handle concepts intelligently; but there are simple people for whom academic or ecclesiastical status serves as a credential testifying to intellectual reliability. We have perhaps taken too little care of this. We have perhaps been too ready to leave such simple people nakedly exposed to the corruptions of unreason issuing from men whose understanding does not match their responsibilities and whose infirmity in the ways of reason and understanding is unluckily accompanied by an urge to argue in public.

This problem—which is by no means peculiar to the field of theology—is being aggravated to-day by the accelerating expansion of our educational system, the increased demand for books, and the apparent lowering of minimum standards of logic and literacy demanded by even reputable publishing houses. Thus, if a book has the "sensational" appeal which mass journalism makes, it can get into print even though it may abound in contradictions, *non sequiturs*, and verbiage which reflects a mental background of conceptual anarchy. Now, you can *correct* a writer who indulges in this kind of thing, but you cannot *argue* with him—at least not until correction has been understood and accepted. Every teacher knows how difficult it is to handle together, in one and the same discussion group, students who are equipped to argue and students whose development is such that they need correction, instruction, and mental discipline before argument can properly begin. This is the kind of situation which has made amicable controversy in the religious field very difficult to achieve of late. Contradictions, *non sequiturs*, conceptual confusion, and semantic misunderstanding present us, of course, with problems of literacy rather than of theology. They call for patient help rather than for lofty rebuke. Yet care for simple-minded readers would seem to require us to deal magisterially with offending writers. Here is an immediate, urgent moral problem. One would like to see it engaging the earnest attention of our new moralists.

But we must not be deflected from our main theme—the temporal claustrophilia of pseudo-theology. One is tempted to speculate that developments in space-research and the consequent problems of what we call the space-age have something to do with the current neglect of the problem of time in theological thinking. I have already said that there is no such neglect of time in the work of creative writers. On the contrary, the subject of time has been a key theme of major twentieth-century literature. In seeking an explanation of this difference, one notes that there is much in recent theological controversy to suggest that in this field the fashionable vogue for space-talk has exercised a mesmeric spell. Under its influence every conceivable intellectual naïvety has been committed, from the suggestion that the increasing exploration of space leaves less and less room in the cosmos for heaven—and even for God—to the popularizations of pretentious by-play with spatial terms like *height* and *depth*, *inside* and *outside*, *up* and *down*.

One of the by-products of this unbalanced space-consciousness has been the apparently increasing hold upon our thinking of a "cross-section" model of the present. The more we picture our world as small and slight among the massive stellar galaxies, and the more we picture ourselves as packed tight on this lonely little overpopulated planet, the falser perhaps becomes the concept of our human status in the universe. A more conscious awareness of the dimension of time would correct this concept. Spatially speaking, you and I take up precious little room in the scheme of things: temporally speaking, you and I assume a rather more significant place in the scheme of things. Two dozen people, edge to edge, can be pressed into quite a small room. But two dozen people laid end to end in time occupy a long period. That is to say, if the lives of two dozen people are laid end to end, births touching deaths, and those people live an average life of sixty years, then their linked life-spans take us back from the year 1965 to A.D. 525. Thirty-six such life-spans would take us back from to-day to the birth of our Lord in Bethlehem. Indeed, if records had been kept on a sufficient scale during the last two thousand years, it would presumably not be difficult to point to as few as two dozen men who each lived eighty years and whose linked life-spans cover the whole period from our Lord's birth to the publication of this morning's newspaper. A sense of the individual man's extension through time is a salutary corrective both to the sense of insignificance which space-consciousness is apt to produce in us, and to the over-weighting of contemporaneousness which fashionable heresies feed on and cultivate.

The current misreading of the significance of time is made up of the false sense of the isolation of the present from the past together with the false notion that the future will give meaning to the present. On the basis of these two self-deceptions, equally inimical to Christian teaching, heresy establishes an apparent strength in our midst which is totally disproportionate to its real power. Thus heresy attempts and achieves in some quarters a demoralization of the faithful which a proper estimate of the nature of time would have forestalled. Let us consider exactly what happens.

Diluters of the faith make great play with such smother phrases as "Many Christians now believe that . . ." or "A considerable number of Anglicans would now agree that . . ." They then introduce propositions which Christians throughout the centuries have firmly rejected. A false numerical strength is imaged on behalf of some new/old heresy by the trick of pretending that the past is *dead*, that our ancestors are no more, that their beliefs no longer matter. Our ancestors in the faith are ruled out of count. The staggering ease with which heretics manage to lead honest, simple Christians into argument on the totally false assumption that all members of the Church now dead are truly, finally, utterly extinguished as beings, so that they do not need to be numbered among the living even when questions of the nature of the Church or the nature of God are at issue, is a frightening testimony to our intellectual corruptibility.

It is horrifying to stumble in discussion or in reading on a Churchman, perhaps even a priest or a bishop, who, when he says, "The Church as a whole . . ." apparently means *that little bit of it* which happens to be on earth in time at this particular moment. He seems to have no idea that he has mentally cut through a living organism, and is now surveying a cross-section which may well represent one of the thinnest or least healthy portions of the whole body extended in time. Obviously a controversialist who by the word "Church" habitually means only that part of it now existing on earth has not begun to think christianly at all. He has yet to learn his Christian alphabet. Small wonder that he is likely, after such a beginning, to proceed to formulate ideas expressive of misunderstanding in the doctrinal, moral, or liturgical field. He has not understood the doctrines he preaches or the liturgy he daily uses, if he has never achieved that basic consciousness of the Church as a community bestriding the centuries which enables more instructed Christians to keep a sense of proportion about the aberrations of the immediate present. A sentence beginning "The Church as a whole believes . . ." could never be checked simply by reference to that bit of the Church now walking between life and death on the earth. Name your favourite Christian saints and writers of the past. Are you prepared to see them cut out of the reckoning, accounted of less moment in the present controversy than any anonymous Yes, No, or Don't Know encountered casually this morning in the street? What presumption would it be that we of this decade, of this year, should arrogate to ourselves the right to pronounce "The Church as a whole believes . . ." on the basis of a quick check-up of current notions. Are we to substitute for the faith of the saints a creed modifiable week by week by reference to an ecclesiastical public opinion poll?

In fact, of course, the Church's liturgy itself serves to keep always in the Christian's mind the awareness of his belonging to a family whose members, whether "living" or "dead", are united in worship and love. With angels and archangels and with all the company of heaven we join together to laud and magnify the glorious Name. Of what significance is it to us that, on this particular occasion, at this particular time, there are but half a dozen of us, or thirty of us, or a hundred of us, gathered together for the breaking of bread and for prayers, when these acts themselves unite us with millions who have repeated them daily throughout the centuries and now gather unseen at our side?

Consider the implications of this supra-temporal character of the Church. The question, How many people joined in worship to-day? is unanswerable by head-counting unless we remove essential Christian presuppositions from our calculations in advance. The question, What percentage of Anglicans assents firmly to every proposition of the Nicene Creed? is a very different question faced christianly in terms of the supra-temporal Church and answered from a poll taken among all who currently label themselves "C of E".

This point needs to be hammered home. We have more than once seen, of late years, an encounter between timeless Catholic orthodoxy and ephemeral peripheral aberration dignified with the name of a "debate", as though the encounter were a dialogue between voices of comparable status and credentials. It would be impossible to sustain such an illusion, even in the popular press, were there a lively sense among Christians of the true nature of time and the place of the Church within it. Before a balanced awareness of the supra-temporal Church, guarding the same truth in all ages, the transient significance of this year's excursions into pseudo-theology shrinks to the dimensions of a pinprick on a planet. We must learn the lesson of our own suddenly revealed capacity to be shocked and outraged by theological aberration. No doubt the emotional disturbance in our response was partly due to the genuine indignation which the dissemination of error among the simple must always justifiably arouse. But was it not also due in part to the fact that we ourselves are victims of the current misassessment of time? We too have thought the contemporary more important in the Church's life than it is. Had we not done so, the existence of pockets of heresy about us would have rippled the surface of our Christian confidence and composure less angrily.

No intellectual tyranny is more confining than the tyranny of the popular *Zeitgeist*. Against no other intellectual influence does the Christian need to be more constantly on guard. The Christian's sense of unity with those who have lived in earlier ages is one of his strongest safeguards against the ever-present temptation to be swept away on the current of fashion. No informed Christian should need to be reminded how richly both the Old and the New Testaments are soaked in the sense of unity enfolding past and present. Present revelation fulfils the wisdom of the past: it does not overturn or obliterate it. It is in the light of a continuous historic experience, stretching back through time to the birth of our Lord in Bethlehem, and further back still through the events recorded in the Old Testament, that the Christian takes his stand of commitment to Christ and his Church. The Christian cannot take an axe in hand to deal with tradition without ceasing to be a Christian. The supra-temporal stability of the Christian Church is a part of its essential character. The Christian is never one for whom Christian belief stands perpetually in the dock, under judgement, over against the accepted values and criteria of contemporary fashion. Rather the Christian is one for whom contemporary values and criteria, notions and attitudes, stand perpetually in the dock, under judgement, over against the supra-temporal stability of the Christian Faith.

A theme of this book—to be further explored later on—is that the view of life we hold will be determined by the kind of data we accept as being truly representative of the universe we inhabit and the state of being in which we share. Our philosophy will be so devised as to accommodate the particular events and experiences we encounter, directly or indirectly, which strike us as truly expressive of the underlying character and purpose of the universe. For instance, if war and strife and destruction strike a man as more truly expressive of the underlying character and purpose of the universe and of life within it, than do happiness and harmony and love, then that man will adopt a negative, pessimistic, or cynical philosophy. He will then try to bring all his experiences into subordinate, if not corroborative, relationship to that philosophy. Similarly, if the state of society in our own day strikes us as more surely expressive of the underlying character and purpose of the universe than any other revelation accorded to us through thought and study, we shall logically and indeed necessarily try to bring our beliefs into accord with the presuppositions and dominant notions of that society. In other words, if the age of the traffic jam, the jet plane, television, high-pressure advertising, nuclear physics, psycho-analysis, lung-cancer, alcoholism, and mass mental derangement seems to us to represent a breakthrough from darkness to light, from ignorance and obscurantism to wisdom and understanding, we shall properly allow the prevalent impulses and insights expressed in this civilization a heavy weight of influence in moulding our beliefs, in determining our overall conception of the nature of reality.

But how many of us believe that the insights productive of and prevalent in the civilization that confronts us are worthy of such high esteem? And—a more important question for the progressives—what reason have we to believe that the values popularly cherished in that civilization are going to carry weight in a hundred years' time?

We must try to be tolerant over this issue. Those exponents of liberal theology who are urgently anxious to trim the Christian Faith to the demands of popular current thinking have a perfect right to believe that the decade of the pop-singer, the Kinsey

Report, the traffic-snarl, and orbiting hardware, represents the fullest realization yet attained to by man of the true nature and purpose of the universe. Believing so—if indeed they so believe —they must logically try to adjust their philosophy at all points to the mentality which has produced and takes delight in these manifestations of the march of progress. In this situation it would be appropriate for them to take over current secularism's notion of the human norm—of what I shall later define in greater detail as "basic man"—and load on to him as much "Christian" trimming as his frame seems capable of carrying without collapse: that is, assuming that their *a priori* admiration for current civilization and the insights it represents has left them with any Christian trimmings unconsigned to the waste paper basket.

Orthodoxy's position is far different. We are convinced that there is something eminently rational in treating as of especially valid significance those events and experiences which have recurred throughout the centuries, in men and women of immensely varied background and understanding, establishing the unfailing and unchanging relevance to personal need of the faith once delivered to the saints. Reason and history combine to assure us that it will be precisely the *unchanging* experience and insight which will bear surest testimony to the underlying character and purpose of the totality compounded of the universe and ourselves. The thing that seized St Paul, St Augustine, and John Donne is obviously the same thing that seized, shall we say, Thomas Merton and C. S. Lewis. It is also obviously the same thing that has now seized my near neighbour, Mrs X. And it is the *sameness* that speaks clearly to the rest of us of the character of the scheme of things in which God has involved us. The *differences* between the recorded personal experiences of these converts are of much less significance as inductive evidence for purposes of this argument, richly important though they may be in other ways.

In short, what is essentially new, novel, or "progressive" is always by its nature suspect in the pure theological field. Terms like "modernist" and "liberal" and "progressive" in the doctrinal sphere are virtually synonymous with "untrustworthy", if not with "heretical". And this statement, provocative as it may seem to some, does not represent a personal point of view, extreme, conservative, bigoted, obscurantist, or what you will. Rather it constitutes a reaffirmation of the nature of time and its relationship to the eternal as universally accepted in Catholic Christendom and as summed up in the doctrine of the Ascension.

Scepticism explicitly rejects this view of the nature of time and its relationship to the eternal. Secularism implicitly rejects it. The pseudo-theology of recent liberal Christianity, a notable phenomenon of our age, represents a fruitless and irrational attempt to range the Church behind the powerful forces of scepticism and secularism, behind the dominant impulses expressed in our mass social culture. It tries to give current unbelief the backing of "Christianity". The attempt will fail: of that we can be sure. But, even in failing, it may prove costly in terms of human suffering. (Already one is meeting the first generation of men and women who have lost their faith and their bearings under the direct "missionary" influence of the "new theology".) And among all the ironies of the present religious situation, not the least of them is this: that the defection of liberal theologians to the banners of our secular civilization and its implicit philosophy of progress should have occurred just at the time when the civilization and its philosophy have come most heavily under judgement in the eyes of those who represent our modern literary culture at the finest point of its development.

Not that the Churchman can ever come to terms with those writers, however penetrating and profound, whose protest against life's absurdity is final and comprehensive. At times this chapter has turned in some sympathy to the critique of contemporary civilization presented to us by twentieth-century literature, so that in conclusion it is perhaps necessary to forestall possible misunderstanding on this point. The Christian Faith is life-affirming, a religion of joy, good news, and inner peace. Nothing which is said in this book should be taken as pointing to any other view than that. Nothing should be understood as being depreciative of the natural order in which God has placed us for our lives in time. The Christian sets the highest value on the natural precisely because its vocation is to be transfigured by the supernatural—and because the natural can become dangerous to us if this transfiguration is not effected. The Christian sees the highest significance in human culture and civilization precisely because these achievements are meant to be vehicles by which God's purposes are worked out here in time—and because, if they are not so used, they become the furniture of Hell.

Only a simpleton, therefore (or perhaps a hostile reviewer), will be able to write of my work, "Mr Blamires drives a wedge between the secular and the religious. This will not do, for God is concerned with human life as a whole, not just with that little bit of it which we call 'religion'." It is precisely *because* God is concerned with life as a whole that one must bring under critical scrutiny any area of modern life to which he is being denied access. What we mean when we speak of "modern secularism" is that vast region of human achievement to which God's creature's are denying him full access, by refusing him an entry into their conscious thoughts and purposes, by excluding personal consecration and faith from the bases of their motivation.

If a doctor wrote a book, *Disease in the Modern World*, or, shall we boldly say, *A Defence of Health*, we should think but poorly of the critic who would write, "Dr X has made a most dangerous distinction between health and disease. This will not do. All men should be healthy all the time, not just some of the time. There is therefore no place for a book which would drive a wedge between sickness and health." You will not get rid of the purely secular outlook by merely repeating that everything good is of God. You will not get rid of worldliness by pretending that it does not exist, any more than you will get rid of disease by pretending that it does not exist. Talk of "holy worldliness" is no doubt well-intentioned, but such talk is semantically and theologically unhelpful—as talk of "healthy disease" would be semantically and medically unhelpful. It is necessary to say this because what is basically a mode of thinking peculiar to Christian Science is in danger of corrupting the Church through the influence of those who seem to imagine that penetrating analysis of current secularism manufactures what in fact it merely identifies. Clearly to diagnose a condition is not to recommend its continuance.

Thus diagnosis of the sickness of a world that shuts itself off from God can never be construed as denigration of the natural or the human. To plead, as orthodoxy does, for a present filled full of the eternal, for natural activity transfigured at every point by supernatural orientation, for a humanity wholly possessed by the divine initiative, is to claim for the whole sphere of natural human achievement a richness and a significance which current liberal theology, for all its protestations to the contrary, never allows to it. For whereas acceptance of the present is essentially life-affirming, the intellectual stretching forward towards a future in which at last man will be fully grown up and the Church can really come to be, is life-denying. It cannot be too often repeated that reduction of the status of the past or of the present to that of a mere *pathway* to the future is essentially life-denying: life-denying for the men and women of ten centuries back, for the men and women of two centuries back, of ten years back, of yesterday, of to-day—life-denying for all except those who will exist on earth in a future which never, never becomes the present. Theological liberalism's idolatry of the future is always thus life-denying. Orthodoxy is life-affirming. Dogmatism, institutionalism, and sacramentalism are life-affirming in that they fill the present full of richness, meaning, and the surety of trust.

44

I have had cause already to refer to what is perhaps the finest literary utterance of our age—T. S. Eliot's *Four Quartets*. Here you will find the sharpest criticism of the contemporary blending with the profoundest estimate of the significance of the present. Eliot's poem revolves around acceptance of the present as the point of intersection of the timeless with time. It brings together the dogmatic and the mystical, the institutional and the personal, the sacramental and the disciplinary, in a pattern of Christian exploration which affirms life so powerfully, so strenuously, that by comparison the anti-supernaturalists, in both the theological and the literary fields, are apt to look like thin-blooded puritans desperately clutching at other people's cast-off garments to hide their nakedness and their anaemia. What could affirm life more comprehensively than Eliot's precise yet all-embracing reconciliation of flux and pattern, change and stability, movement and fixity, time and eternity, darkness and light, the way of the fire and the way of the rose? At the heart of the reconciliation, philosophically and historically, dogmatically and personally, is the Word made flesh. The great archetypal moments of the Christian Revelation—Annunciation, Incarnation, Crucifixion, Resurrection—are central to the pattern of history and must be reproduced centrally in the lives of each of us to give shape and meaning to our temporal course. Is Eliot's poetic re-statement of this simple yet profound Christian truth a piece of dogmatism or a personal existential testimony? The answer, of course, is that it is *both at once*. It is both inseparably. When the really profound and searching truth is uttered, the truly overwhelming Christian experience lived through and recorded, it turns out to be an inextricably unified web from which the dogmatic element can never be disentangled. To try to divest the poetry of an Eliot, the conversion record of a St Augustine or a C. S. Lewis, of its authoritative dogmatic content would be like trying to dehydrate a reservoir.

Eliot's moments of illumination and contemplation, moments

in which time is transcended, moments in and out of time, are instances of that ever-living present through which the divine effects its "takeover" of the human. The takeover must be complete. It involves the whole man and the whole of life. This means that the human intellect as well as the will and the heart will be involved in one unified pattern of commitment. We shall see later on how inconsistent and irrational it is to withhold the intellect from the full unified offering, here and now, by which the human is involved with the divine. The full human offering is always God's demand of man. Man cannot answer it if he tries to keep a special corner for human self-sufficiency in the field of understanding.

3

Dogmatism and Liberalism

*What is the key difference between
the dogmatist and the liberal?*

The key difference between the dogmatist and the liberal is not
properly summed up by saying that the dogmatist thinks he possesses and understands the truth, while the liberal prefers to sus-
pend judgement. It is misleading to say that the dogmatist claims
that we human beings really *know* the truth, while the liberal
more modestly denies that we know. The key difference is that
the liberal believes that we human beings are progressively learning the truth, in other words are *going to get to know* the truth,
while the dogmatist believes that nothing of the kind is happening. The dogmatist believes that, theologically speaking, men are
not going to get to know on earth anything of crucial importance
that we do not know already. The dogmatist believes that the
delicate balance of our knowledge and our ignorance in the
religious field is precisely the situation designed for us by God
himself, and that fundamentally it does not change from century
to century. The dogmatist believes that God indeed overrules;
that he has put us in our present situation in the sense that he has
told us what we need to know and no more. Believing this, the
dogmatist looks on what God has already told us with the
maximum of respect and reverence. The revelation of the truth
which God has given us is the life-line thrown out from eternity
into time. It has been thrown out because God loves us. It has
the degree of clarity and simplicity which it has because God

loves us and will not leave us in the dark. It has also, at the intellectual level, the element of "uncertainty" which it has, because God loves us and therefore will never compel us.

*What, from the dogmatist's point of view,
is the position of the liberal?*

From the dogmatist's point of view, the position of the liberal may be represented thus: "We are gradually discovering the truth about human life and its relationship to the beyond (if the beyond indeed exists). We are gradually learning what God is like and what he is about (that is, if he indeed exists). There is going to be a happy time when we *know* these things. It is all a question of our increasing in knowledge and understanding. We have learned quite a lot already from past students of theology— that is, from the prophets of the Old Testament, the disciples of Christ, the evangelists, the early fathers, the schoolmen, the reformers, and so on. We have learned from them positively, and we have learned from them negatively through the mistakes they naturally made because they had the misfortune to live in unenlightened days before modern science and modern philosophy and modern psychology got to work. New developments in these fields have made a vast difference to our own progress in the theological field. We may appear to have gone backward rather than forward, in that we have greater cause than ever to doubt the truths of the Christian Faith as generally accepted by believers in the past, but we are not so naïve as to believe that we cannot make progress in reverse gear."

What, by contrast, is the position of the dogmatist?

The position of the dogmatist is this. We are not intended to *know* the nature and purposes of God in the same way that we know how a motor car engine works and when the next eclipse of the sun will be. We are finite creatures with brains specially adapted to study and reflection within the space–time framework which we inhabit during our span on earth. But God has made us aware of the eternity outside this framework, for which we are destined and to which we essentially belong. Moreover he has given us, in time, a revelation of himself and his purposes so rich in itself that we could spend life-times studying it, exploring it, and for ever receiving new illumination from it. But these illuminations will not fundamentally alter the character of the human situation—man in time reaching out to an eternity incomprehensible to the temporal. The revelation given us through the prophets, the evangelists, the fathers, and the centuries of Christian witness, above all through our Lord himself, is of God's *giving*, not of man's *discovering*. That our minds are not up to understanding it fully is in part no fault of our own: we are finite creatures of mingled brain and brawn, not pure intelligences: it is also in part our fault, in that we misinterpret through eyes often blinded by passion, vanity, uncharity, or sloth. But the thing which is of God's giving, testified to through the ages in the lives and teaching of saints and martyrs, is itself of course irrefutable. The Church preserves that irrefutable truth and will continue to preserve it because it is a divinely established institution. Individual Churchmen will get it wrong: we shall all, mere fallible men and women, get it somewhat wrong in our diverse ways. We shall misunderstand and misinterpret, falsely elaborate here, falsely dilute there. But the truth will not be lost, not be taken away, not be permanently damaged, as long as the Church continues to be the Church, the body of men and women trying to live in our Lord.

Thus there is still plenty of brainwork to do. There will always be plenty of brainwork to do, in ensuring that the central deposit of truth is not blurred by confusion or overlaid by irrelevancies, in exploring the immensely varied implications of this all-relevant truth to the changing situations of different centuries and different regions and different cultures. There will always be plenty of brainwork to do in high-lighting aspects of the truth more particularly applicable to the need of the moment, in correcting excessive emphases and pressing converse ones.

Which therefore of the two, dogmatist or liberal,
adopts the more confident posture?

Superficially it might appear that the dogmatist adopts the more confident posture, in that he points to creeds and traditional doctrinal formulations as embodying unquestionable truths. But the dogmatist's confidence is in that which is given of God. His recourse to this source of confidence is the result of his deep lack of confidence in the capacity of the human understanding to explore the infinite and to discover by inquiry what is the nature of God. The liberal has no such reticence. The liberal is committed to a human inquiry in the theological field whose end is the knowledge of God. The liberal therefore presupposes that man's intellect is capable of making progress in this field by virtue of the same kind of competence that enables it to make progress in the study of science or the development of technology. The liberal thus makes greater claims for man's intellect than does the dogmatist. The liberal's posture is, in this sense, more confident than the dogmatist's.

Which of the two, dogmatist or liberal,
adopts the more creaturely attitude
towards the mysteries of God?

Superficially it might appear that the liberal adopts the more creaturely attitude towards the mysteries of God, in that he lays great stress on the "uncertainty" of established traditions and doctrinal formulations. He regards propositions, which frame the faith, tentatively and speculatively. He claims that scholars are as yet only *on the way* to the discovery of religious truth. Anything like clear formulation of religious truth, such that it can call forth general and unambiguous Christian assent, lies far ahead of us in the future.

The liberal, therefore, insists that the dogmatist's attachment to intellectual formulations of the faith in the form of established doctrines represents an uncreaturely presumption before the mystery of the eternal. But this is an erroneous and shallow inference. For the liberal's tentativeness before the truths given in revelation represents virtually a rejection of revelation. Revelation is the lifeline thrown out by the Creator to the creature. The liberal's refusal to cling to the lifeline is related to the presupposition that no lifeline is needed, that the creature can find his own way, intellectually speaking. The liberal's undervaluing of revelation on its intellectual side, and his consequent overvaluing of the humanly directed pursuit of truth, constitute a refusal to accept the limitations of the human situation. By contrast, it is the dogmatist's full and frank facing of the limitations of human thinking which compels him to snatch at the divine lifeline with unquestioning joy and confidence. The dogmatist accepts that man's ignorance, face to face with the divine, is not an ephemeral feature of a few particularly dark centuries which will eventually be superseded by centuries of fully verified and scientifically accredited knowledge of religious truth. Rather the dogmatist accepts man's ignorance of the divine, in terms of inductive verification, as precisely designed for him by God. In short, the dogmatist does not believe that we are in an abandoned situation out of which we must fumblingly grope our way to the light. The dogmatist accepts the human situation for what it is, under Providence. God, he believes, means it to be thus and thus. It is, in different senses, at different times, for different moods, tragic, comic, ironic: but it is always, as it confronts us minglingly with the knowable and the unknowable, the verifiable and the unverifiable, essentially the working out of God's purposes for us.

The liberal virtually refuses to accept the human situation for what it is. The individual liberal may be a man of such piety, sanctity, and heroic self-sacrifice, that most Christians, at his side, would stink like sepulchres. But in so far as he intellectually refuses to accept the human situation for what it is, he is involved in an uncreaturely rebellion against God's will. In truth, therefore, the dogmatist adopts the more creaturely attitude towards the mysteries of God.

Which of the two, dogmatist or liberal,
holds before our eyes the more convincing image of God
as the God of Love?

Superficially it is sometimes made to appear that the liberal holds the more convincing image of God as the God of Love. Certainly the liberal himself often believes that this is one of his strongest cards in dispute with the dogmatist. But it is not difficult to show, on several counts, that the liberal's claim in this respect is erroneous.

When the dogmatist presses the case for propositional clarity in relation to fundamental doctrines of the Church—the Incarnation, the Redemption, the Ascension, the Holy Trinity—the liberal is apt to reply, "These intellectual formulations are all very well, but we must remember that God is not an object of intellectual inquiry but a God of Love". This familiar argument appears in various forms. It rests upon an assumed but concealed antithesis between love and reason, between loving and knowing or understanding. This antithesis, once brought to light, can be shown to be invalid. But the liberal tends to resent bringing it to light and is apt to cite the attempt to bring it to light as an instance of intellectual activity inappropriate to the consideration of a God of Love. In short, a good deal of confusion is caused in the theological field by the trick (it *is* a trick) of making use of the human intellect for the purpose of saying "God is Love" and then denying the applicability of intellectual criteria to the further examination of that proposition which has already been established by an intellectual act.

There is, of course, no antithesis between love and reason, between loving and knowing. But it is easy to nourish in uneducated or mentally indisciplined people the vague feeling that such an antithesis exists and has validity. It is easy because of the very nature of our daily lives and because of certain accidental developments in our use of words. We are accustomed to use the word *love* in contexts with which intellectual pursuits have very little direct connection. In particular the word is most strongly associated with sexual relationships, family relationships (especially those between mother and young child), and charitable activities touching the poor, the afflicted, the defective, the lonely, and the miserable. In short the word *love* is most frequently brought to mind in relation to situations where comfort, compassion, tenderness, sympathy, and practical physical (or even financial) help are most properly called into play; situations most remote from those in which demands upon the intellect are made with any degree of priority. Similarly the word *knowledge* is most frequently used in relation to situations which scarcely overlap at all with those in relation to which the word *love* is most likely to be brought into play. The word *knowledge* brings to the minds of most of our fellows the world of schools, colleges, and universities, of libraries, encyclopedias, and textbooks, of examinations and degrees.

Against the background of "natural" mental associations, it is easy to nourish the false notion that love and reason, or knowledge, stand in some kind of mutually antithetical relationship. But of course it is not so. Quite the contrary. As every student of language must be aware, there is even an ancient verbal connection between the act of intellectually penetrating to the heart of a problem and the act of physically penetrating a woman in sexual intercourse. For both acts the verb *to know* is used in the Bible. There is neither incongruity nor antithesis between the pursuit of the maximum intellectual clarity and precision on the one hand, and the cultivation of affection and devotion on the other hand. On the contrary, there is a deeply harmonious relationship between the intellect's fierce pursuit of clear knowledge and understanding, and the pursuit of the heart's desire which we call love. When a scientist is busy with his microscope in his laboratory, he is too preoccupied to give much thought to his girl friend's charms. When he is embracing his girl friend in the meadow, we trust he is likewise too preoccupied to give much thought to the uncompleted experiment and calculations awaiting him back at the laboratory. These two images represent an appropriate division of human interests, but they do not represent a schizophrenic personality involved in mutually antithetical activities.

The dogmatist has two arguments against the liberal's case, which are directly based upon his conviction that God is a God of Love. In the first place, the dogmatist believes that the lifeline of revelation expresses God's concern for his creatures positively. In the second place, he believes that God has chosen the way of the lifeline (no doubt among other reasons) precisely because he will not leave his world abandoned—even intellectually abandoned—though he will preserve its freedom none the less. God, being a God of Love, will not be represented by truths of such a kind that they are attainable by the brainy man but not by the dunderhead. God, being a God of Love, will not be represented by truths of such a kind that they are clearly understandable by fully educated Christians in the thirtieth century, dimly and confusedly discernible to but a few forward-looking theologians in the twentieth century, and hopelessly misread by faithful Christians in the tenth century.

God's love is plainly discernible to the dogmatist in the way that faith is open to all, understanding of God's truths equally on offer to all, and propositional representation of his truths capable of being made on a variety of levels so as to match virtually any degree of dullness or scholarship. Thus the *Oxford Dictionary of the Christian Church*'s definition of the Incarnation as being "opposed to all theories of a mere theophany" and as asserting "an abiding union in the Person of Christ of Godhead and

Manhood without the integrity or permanence of either being impaired" represents a propositional exploration on a level of utterance to which certain levels of intelligence are adjusted of a truth which we present to children and simple people by saying that Jesus, the child of the Virgin Mary, was the Son of God.

For the dogmatist God's love is plainly discernible in the lifting of fundamental credal truth out of the stream of ever-moving, ever-changing human ideas, which shift and fluctuate with the shifting of intellectual fashion and the ebb and flow of human understanding, and the planting of it four-square out of the reach of controversy, way above the level on which quarrels flourish and bitterness is bred. It is therefore painful to the dogmatist when he sees his fellow-Christians trying to give to guaranteed truths the status of opinions over which strife can fitly arise. It is painful because, among other things, the attempt seems to represent God as having given us so much less than he has in fact given us, as having left us in the dark when he has in fact lit the firmament of understanding with lights, as having abandoned his world, when in truth his love is about us in the very nourishment offered to our minds by the teaching of his Church. It is thus the dogmatist who more convincingly holds before men's eyes the image of God as a God of Love.

Even though the immediate question at issue has been answered, it would be inappropriate, in view of recent controversy, to turn from this subject without adding some further points. So much misuse has lately been made of the sentence "God is Love" that much time is going to be needed to repair the damage done. I have already referred to the sleight of argument by which this sentence is used to smother rational discourse, and which depends upon an unidentified and wholly mischievous notion that there is some fundamental discongruity between the sphere of reason and the sphere of love. There is another mischievous notion abroad, which is vague, blurred, difficult to pin down, and yet familiar to all who take note of what is being said in the theological field either at the academic or at the journalistic level. I can best define this notion as one that sentimentalizes "love" so as to imply a fundamental incongruity between love and law, or between love and discipline, or between love and clarity of thought, or even between love and the existence of any kind of discomfort and unpleasantness in the universe.

We have got to bring a rigorous scrutiny to bear upon current usages of the word *love* (and perhaps even more importantly, *Love*) in the theological field. One has read books or articles in which great play is made with statements such as that God is Love, or that Love is the Ultimate Reality, or that Love lies at the ground of all being. These statements may be unexceptional in themselves and yet they may be accompanied by overtones which turn them into dangerously misleading generalizations. Again, they may be misleading because they stand *un*accompanied by overtones which would correct and forestall natural misunderstanding.

Thus, if a book makes much of the proposition that God is Love, we cannot rightly judge its theological quality unless we gather together all the threads in the book which together weave for the mind a *picture* of love. To take an extreme example; if you were to write a book on the love-lives of numerous oft-married film-stars, you would not turn the thing into a sound piece of theology by periodically inserting reminders that God himself is Love. Even though the statement about God is itself unexceptional, its context renders it improper and misleading. Something very like this has in fact been happening in recent pseudo-theology on a less sensational and less obvious, but perhaps therefore more pernicious plane. One reads in a book that Love is the Ground of all things, that Love is the Ultimate that human understanding can reach, that God himself is Love, and yet in the rest of the book the word *love* is used exclusively in contexts which relate to the intimate or cosy contact of person with person, perhaps jolly, perhaps erotic, but essentially enjoyable and uncluttered by any of the harsher realities of life. Of course *nothing is said* plainly touching this issue. But the overtones of the book are such as to conjure up, in connection with the word *love*, images of lovers staring into each other's eyes, of mothers suckling babies, of welcoming smiles in dancing eyes as wanderers return or parted families gather for Christmas celebrations.

I do not think I am being unfair in arguing thus. I have myself had cause to try to reason with people infected with the voguish simplification which would reduce all theology to the statement, *God is Love*, and thereby abolish doctrine and law, and I have myself been astonished to see the astonishment registered in their own eyes when I have said, "Now I will go a good way with you in this argument if you will first accept my dictum that in so far as love has been expressed in my own life during the last fortnight, it was essentially when I wiped the vomit from the children's bedroom floor in the middle of the night so as to save my wife the trouble of getting out of bed, and when, visiting bedridden Granny Smith, I emptied her bedpan and cleaned it with disinfectant. (The examples are of course imaginary. I can claim the virtue of neither of them.) Both were loathsome duties, properly hateful, destructive of and inimical to life's joy and beauty, and the fewer times I have to repeat them during my course on earth, the better it pleases me. I take it that this is roughly what you are getting at when you tell me that *God is Love*. I press the point because I am not keen myself on abstractions, like *Love* with a capital L, as predicated of God. I like to express myself concretely about these things, and above all to bring religious thought down from the clouds and make it truly relevant to the daily lives of ordinary men and women. You would agree with me that toilsome, unpleasant, tedious, even disgusting duties like these are probably the surest acts of love we perform, and that is the kind of act you have in mind when you say that God is Love, or that Love lies at the base of things?"

At the human level it is always likely to be evasive to talk about Love in the abstract. Reference to concrete acts of love is necessary to ensure that discussion does not lose itself in unreality. Of course no instructed Christian ought to need to be reminded about what we mean by the statement, God is Love. The crucifix exists to ensure that we shall not forget. And any talk about God being Love which overlooks the Cross misses the heart of the matter. Likewise any talk about love at the human level which neglects suffering falsifies by default.

Thus one cannot protest too strongly against the modish chatter of recent pseudo-theology which has often preoccupied itself ostensibly with Love, while omitting reference to the disciplines, austerities, rigours, and self-sacrifices in which love, at the human level, is most finely expressed. To neglect these and, at the same time, to scatter one's talk or writing with overtones which associate the joys of companionship, congeniality, and shared erotic intimacy with the word *love*, is to present, by misemphasis, a totally misleading account of Christian love. Though every individual statement may be true, christianly considered, the total argument to which these statements contribute may, by sheer unbalance, constitute a travesty of Christian teaching. Moreover it will constitute exactly the kind of travesty likely to corrupt men and women at their most corruptible. We do not need a horned devil, scattering lies, to lead us astray. A theologian, speaking selected truths, can do it just as easily.

It is indeed an act of love when I stare into the eyes of the girl I have chosen and tell her how beautiful she is. It is an even finer act of love when I look into the eyes of my aged, vain, pompous, garrulous, egotistical acquaintance and pretend heroically, by the half-hour, that he is not boring me to death with his tedious and endlessly repetitive reminiscences. And do not tell me that I have only to listen long enough and patiently enough, and his talk will one day grow delightful to me. Life is too short for that. No doubt there is a sympathy that can grow, under God, in the heart of the patient listener, as acres of time are washed over by floods of empty garrulity, but the sympathy is the fruit of compassion and the kin of pity: there cannot be joy in it. Only the sentimentalist would deny the validity of joyless love.

Which of the two, dogmatism or liberalism,
is more likely to touch the nerve of a sceptical age?

Before I answer this question, let me record two caveats. To prove that a man's views "cut no ice with people to-day" is not to prove that the man's views are false, or even irrelevant. People can be so stupid and ignorant that they turn a deaf ear to the most prophetically relevant truths. Likewise to show that a man's views are really "getting across to the modern world" or really "meeting a demand" does not prove that those views are true or even relevant. Nevertheless, in a book which is a treatment of dogmatism rather than of dogma, it is important to answer the fashionable charge of the liberals that dogmatism makes no appeal to a sceptical age and that in liberalism alone lies hope of bringing Christianity to the hearts of our contemporaries.

In *Letters to Malcolm chiefly on Prayer* C. S. Lewis asks, "By the way, did you ever meet, or hear of, anyone who was converted from scepticism to a 'liberal' or 'de-mythologized' Christianity? I think that when unbelievers come in at all, they come in a good deal further." This certainly accords with my own personal experience. One looks in vain for records of conversion which would corroborate the claim of liberals to be getting into touch with modern scepticism in a fruitful way.

If, as I believe, the dogmatist alone can hope to make an impression on a sceptical generation, it is not difficult to explain why. It is because the dogmatist caters for scepticism as the liberal does not. It is also because dogmatism entertains within its own framework an element of scepticism which is natural to the rational mind and which the liberal tries to obliterate. These last two sentences will sound paradoxical to many readers and, at first sight, outrageously false to others. I must beg such readers to be patient while the points these sentences make are amplified and illustrated.

It is necessary to distinguish between what I shall call "scepticism of the first degree" and "scepticism of the second degree". In order to do so I shall take an analogy (it is *only* an analogy, not an instance, and not an exact parallel) from outside the theological field—from the field of detective fiction. Let us suppose that, at the beginning of a novel, the police are called to a house in which it appears that a man has been murdered. There is the corpse, shot through the heart, but there is no gun to be found. There is evidence of theft and such evidence of the deceased man's involvement in blackmail, vice, and other un-savoury activities as to provide plenty of motivation for murder. There are many witnesses who come along and speak to the police of what they have seen and heard. Finger-prints are found. The gun is discovered. Stories corroborate one another, and the interlocking of all the evidence points quite plainly to two or three suspects. When the police question these suspects, and others who have evidence to offer, they take nothing on trust, they accept nothing as true merely because it is said to them, how-ever genuine and sincere the witness may be. Every statement has to be checked against material evidence and against other statements. Every statement is regarded as potentially false. This is scepticism of the first degree.

Then, of course, along comes the amateur detective. He studies the evidence, ponders, broods, and reveals doubts of a kind which none of the police and few of the book's readers (except the most expert detective fiction fans) have entertained. At first mystified and incredulous, we hear the amateur detective casting doubt on all conclusions so far reached. The most obvious starting-points, the very basic presuppositions, are probed so as totally to alter the picture. Was the deceased necessarily *murdered*? Was the gunshot necessarily the real cause of death? Might there have been an elaborate frame-up designed to bring certain people under suspicion? Is it possible, after all, that the whole thing was rigged? This is scepticism of the second degree. It undercuts first-degree scepticism. When it first makes its appearance, the police in the novel, hard-headed men, well trained in first-degree scepticism, scoff at it. It does not "speak" to them. They are operating mentally (little do they know it) on a much shallower level than the amateur detective. His scepticism has cut away the ground from under their feet so that their earlier painstaking scepticism in regard to X's testimony and Y's testimony now looks petty and trivial. What was the point of being so cleverly sceptical about X's answers and Y's answers when the very framework of assumptions within which questions were put to them proves now to have been itself questionable?

Analogies of this kind must not be pressed too far, nor correspondences too closely identified, but perhaps this illustration will help the liberal theologian to understand what his questioning attitude towards individual Christian doctrines looks like to the dogmatist. The dogmatist, if I am right, has always had his doubts about the Christian Faith—but they have been at the level of second-degree scepticism. The dogmatist, as often as not, has deeply and massively questioned whether there is any truth at all in the Christian Faith, whether there is a God at all, a purpose of any kind in human life, any meaning or design in the total scheme of things, any thing or person that is truly good at the basis of existence. The man who has lived through these doubts, who has come to accept the full rational and existential validity of the Christian Faith, the sheer factual force of the Christian Revelation and its fruits in the lives of men—this man cannot sympathize with scepticism of the first degree. His difficulty has been to accept that God exists, that God loves men, that he has a purpose for men, that he has entered our world in

Christ and saved us. This difficulty overcome, what "difficulty" remains? If God is God, if God became Man, entered this world, established his Church, what should we expect but that the divine touch should lie upon the human scene, manifesting itself in mystery and miracle too deep to comprehend, too marvellous to explain? Yet the dogmatist sees the liberal apparently having no difficulty (no disturbing, no *obsessive* difficulty, that is) with the basic supernatural premises of the Christian Faith—the existence of God, the eternal destiny of man, and even the Incarnation—and yet making heavy weather of every detailed implication of these supernatural premises within the sphere of time. This first-degree scepticism is alien to the dogmatist's thinking and his experience. He suspects it is also alien to the secular sceptic's thinking and experience. He suspects that in this respect he can come to grips with the secular sceptic at a level of mutual sympathy and understanding on which, sad to say, he is never likely to meet his fellow Christians who are infected with the new liberalism.

This is a truly agonizing issue for twentieth-century Christendom, and I am trying to face it honestly, making no attempt to tone down the crisis of mutual confidence within the Church which the split between dogmatist and liberal represents. The dogmatist is as much astonished at the apparent *facility* of the liberal's faith in what he calls the essentials of Christianity as he is at the apparent *difficulty* the liberal has with what follows from those essentials. The dogmatist is overwhelmed by what seems to him a wild inconsistency and disproportion in the liberal's thinking. The inconsistency resides in the ready acceptance of God himself and God in Christ and the parallel reluctance to see God's hand plainly at work in miracle or mystery, in sacrament or sainthood, in book or body. The disproportion resides in the liberal's determination to be for ever trimming the branches when the trunk needs to be defended, to be for ever trying to smooth the edges and blunt the outlines of doctrines and practices deeply embedded in two thousand years of Christian witness and experience, when the questions before our age are God or no God, Christ or no Christ, the coming Kingdom or meaninglessness and annihilation.

We have not finished yet with scepticism of the first degree and scepticism of the second degree. The dogmatist manifests second-degree scepticism in other ways than those just cited. For, as we shall see later in this book, the dogmatist is more sceptical of the reliability of human knowledge than the liberal is, more sceptical about the trustworthiness of human ways of getting to know, and therefore readier to trust (less willing to try to pass judgement on) the fullness of revelation. It is not that the dogmatist is quicker to swallow a certain type of formulation (for example, doctrinal truths couched in propositional form) but rather that the dogmatist is slower to swallow anything, more sceptical of all human formulations and intellectual achievements, and therefore readier to accept the necessary human makeshift. Not because we are going to know better later on: but because we are never going to know in time. Not because the dogmatist mistakes the makeshift for an absolute, the propositional statement for the perfect utterance, but because he has accepted all temporal goods as makeshifts.

Of course the liberal misunderstands the dogmatist in this respect. Hence the liberal continues to speak of the dogmatist as one who finds the "traditional framework of metaphysics" entirely satisfactory, and of himself as one who by contrast is seeking a new and better philosophical framework. The liberal seems incapable of facing the fact that whereas he is aware of the "provisional" nature of the traditional metaphysical framework, the dogmatist is deeply aware of the provisional nature of *all philosophical frameworks*—and that includes the "new and better" philosophical framework which the liberals or their colleagues are going to discover next year or next decade or next century. In the dogmatist's eyes, they are all going to be equally provisional, equally expressive of the limitations of the human intellect.

In intellectual matters—*as in all departments of life and experience*—the dogmatist has come to terms with the provisional nature of finitude, with the makeshiftiness of experience in "this environment of non-achievement which we call time" (Guiton, *Journals*). Human love, fumbling, often blundering through unintentional tactlessness or misunderstanding, is after all a makeshift love. The human family, the human home, for all the happiness found there, have their term, their inevitable defects, which make them, to the supernatural eye, makeshift institutions. Likewise all human knowledge is, in this sense, makeshift knowledge —the best we can do.

But—how important this *but* is—the makeshiftiness is not an ephemeral feature which with effort and study we shall erase from the human scene. The makeshiftiness is something which God has designed for us here below, and our obedience requires us to accept it—accept it gladly. We are not to kick against it resentfully; to pretend that we can turn earthly homes into timeless perfections or the formulations of the human brain into eternal absolutes. God has given us these things because they are what we need. We must neither turn our backs on them nor pretend they are in all respects identical with what awaits us in his kingdom.

I shall not have made my point effectively unless the reader understands that there is a scepticism which makes one, in the long run, sceptical about scepticism. Certainly the dogmatist's second-degree scepticism makes him sceptical of the liberal's first-degree scepticism. But equally second-degree scepticism has a self-destructive function for the logical mind. In the long run it casts doubt upon its own validity. In fact, if I may so put it, scepticism, pursued to its logical conclusion, demands an act of faith so preposterous that scepticism laughs the demands out of court.

This process needs to be illustrated. It may well represent a vital moment of decision in the life of a thoughtful intellectual. Many Christians experience moments of doubt which seem to bring the whole Christian postulate into question. Suppose it were all false! The idea hits us between the eyes, throwing a sudden darkness over all plans, hopes, joys, habits, and consolations. Suppose there were no God, no Father, no Incarnation, no Saviour, no scheme of Redemption, no Church, no Heaven. Suppose all the Christian teachings were based on human delusions and superstitions, a tissue of wish-fulfilling dreams conjured up from the depths of the unconscious as vain compensations for the frustrations and fears of unsatisfied appetites and inhibited egos. Suppose only the physical universe existed, self-created, self-perpetuating, in its long evolutionary history throwing up consciousness as easily as cabbages, immortal longings as readily as dinosaurs or jellyfish. What then? Scepticism presses this question until despair and desolation stare us in the face.

But scepticism, mercifully, does not stop there. It presses further. Suppose this were indeed the case, then you—and millions of human beings like you—have devised and cherished this extraordinary thing called Christianity, by which men have lived and died in hope and joy, in charity and works of mercy, in costly discipline and self-sacrifice. That is to say, they have done these things—the great saints and martyrs of old, the saints of yesterday, the faithful Christians of to-day—because they have corporately invented and sustained a false dream of the origin and meaning and purpose of the universe and the life within it, a dream which we call the Christian Faith. We men and women have invented God, the Trinity, the Incarnate Christ, the Redemption, the Resurrection, the Church, the sacraments. We human beings have invented all this, and crowned it with the vision of Heaven and with a supernatural explanation of things which is alone capable of compensating for, and making sense of, the evil, injustice, and suffering in which so many human lives are clouded.

In short, on this premiss, we have invented something far, far better than the universe itself and all that is in it. Thus scepticism proceeds undeflected upon its ruthlessly logical course until, inevitably, it cries out, "If this Christian Faith is not true, then it *ought* to be!" And so it ought, for it is better than anything that the universe has to offer and is the only thing that can "save God's face", front to front with the mounting record of human misery that history gives us.

"If this Christian Faith is not true, then it ought to be." Scepticism checks itself. "What have I said?" I have said that I know better than the First Cause (if there is one), that I have a compassion and a wisdom which is beyond the reach of whatever source of existence and meaning the universe contains or derives from. I can beat the whole universe at its own game. . . . Scepticism begins to laugh at the fruits of its own reasoning. Scepticism goes a little further and whispers to me, "Is it possible that the logic of your situation as a being who did not manufacture yourself requires you to recognize the following as an equation: *This ought to be = This truly is?* For the alternative seems to be that you should recognize yourself as a God omniscient who knows better than the whole cosmic process what that process should be about."

Thus scepticism, in the long run, laughs itself out of court. It rejects the preposterous act of faith which would make of Christendom and the Christian Faith inventions of man and offshoots of a purposeless cosmic process. It rejects the preposterous act of faith which would make of Harry Blamires the wisest and knowingest thing that evolution has yet thrown up. Scepticism, if it is logical to the end, destroys itself.

It is because of its radical involvement with second-degree scepticism that dogmatism is more effective than liberalism in touching the nerve of a sceptical age.

Which of the two, dogmatism or liberalism,
is more congenial to the scientific mind?

Liberal theology makes much of the necessity to come to terms
with the age of science and of the impossibility of commending
the faith in its traditional dogmatic form to educated products of
that age. Yet there is much to suggest that on this topic a bigger
than usual smokescreen of propaganda is concealing a bigger
than usual mass of hard facts. The facts speak for themselves.
The Roman Catholic Church, with its firm dogmatism, has its
fair share of faithful among eminent men of science. The recently
revived conservative evangelicalism has a following among
scientists, and among doctors perhaps especially, which often
surprises those Christians who find all forms of dogmatism repellent. So far so good. We have evidence that the truly scientific
mind, with a high degree of scholarship, is not necessarily re-
pelled by theological dogmatism.

The climate of opinion, therefore, in which the hazy notion is
kept alive, that there is some kind of deep contradiction between
science and dogmatic theology, needs to be inquired into. Careful
scrutiny of the means and the people by whom this notion is
cherished would, I think, lead us to interesting conclusions. Of
course one cannot pretend to argue here on any basis more solid
than that of personal experience and observation over many
years of acquaintance with religious attitudes in the world of the
educated. But the fruits of such experience and observation are
offered honestly for what they are worth.

To begin with, it is not the scientists who are forever talking
about the difficulty of commending a full dogmatic Christianity
to the age of science. Nor is it, generally speaking, deeply committed Christians. Still less is it those theologians whose breadth
of scholarship and whose keen attachment to logic and coherence
might be supposed to render them most sensitive in this matter.
Indeed, if one is honest, one cannot but note that the theologians
most notable for their scholarship are least prone to contribute to

the talk of there being a crisis, or even a major stumbling-block, for the Church through its confrontation by the scientific world.

It is a totally different stream in our culture from either the genuinely scientific or the genuinely theological that cherishes the pseudo-antithesis between science and theological dogmatism. One must try to characterize this particular stream of thought without appearing to denigrate certain disciplines, and above all without belittling the efforts of men and women in crucial and difficult fields of thought. That being said, it is fair to claim that, if my experience is typical, the pseudo-antithesis between science and theological dogmatism is kept alive in the educational world chiefly by those engaged in teaching such subjects as Psychology, Sociology, Education, the Philosophy of This and the Philosophy of That, and of course Literature. (Since I teach Literature myself, perhaps it can be allowed to me here that I am not necessarily denigrating any of these disciplines.)

One will hear more talk about the clash between scientific and religious modes of thought in a day from men who have no special training either in science or theology than one could hear in a year from the same number of genuine scientists and genuine theologians. And this is not because the scientists are all atheists or agnostics. Far from it. They are as likely to be dogmatically committed Churchmen as they are to be decisive atheists. My experience is that it is from among Science dons that you will draw support for a mission to a university; from among Arts dons that you will draw support for a conference of religion-discussers.

The truth is that the liberal's claim to be able to get in touch with the scientific mind more readily than the dogmatist is based upon a number of false assumptions. One of these false assumptions is the notion that there is an antithesis between faith and reason of such a kind that the more religious truths you invite a person to believe, and the more precisely those truths are framed, the greater the strain you will put on that person's reason. From this it would seem to the liberal to follow that, since scientists are pre-eminently rational men, the more Christian doctrines you put before them for acceptance, the more you will invite them to take intellectual risks which would jeopardize their integrity as men devoted by calling to the scrutiny and establishment of verifiable truth.

But of course the liberal's case collapses if it is established that no conflict exists between faith and reason. For the Christian there can be no such conflict in principle (this is not to say that individuals may not have particular problems which they would honestly, though in ignorance, regard as problems of reconciling the irreconcilable). Indeed, to admit the existence in principle of a contradiction between faith and reason is virtually to declare yourself a non-Christian, or at best an uninstructed Christian, in advance: for it is to claim as your own a problem which unbelief alone can create. Thus, for instance, the evolutionary determinist sees the human reason as a chance product of the natural process: it is nothing more than the consciousness of the animal sustained by memory and foresight and organized, through the finer development of the senses and the brain, into a machine capable of investigating the very order of nature which has given it birth. Such a machine could take no cognizance of a supposed "supernatural" order, and therefore the person in whom such a machine functioned could bring recognition of a supernatural order into operation only by inventing a special faculty capable of contacting it. Such a faculty, granted that it were called faith, would be an irrational thing to have dreamed up, and its hypotheses about the supernatural world would deserve all the scorn poured on them by the materialist psychologists.

But for the Christian, by virtue of the doctrine of divine creation itself, the human reason is the gift of God, which exalts man over the rest of the natural order, rendering him capable, not only of investigating and recording the operation of that order, but also of judging it from the point of view of a higher order into which it does not enter. By declaring man rational, we press the fact that man, a subject belonging in part to another dimension of being and destined for an other-worldly end, is able to find in the objective world a significance of which the objective world itself knows nothing. We press at the same time the power of man to construct and organize concepts whose reality could not be verified by the evidence of the natural order alone. Reason is thus the faculty by which man organizes his response to and acquaintance with the universe in what we call the pursuit of scientific studies. It is also the faculty by which values are conceived, and which thus allows us to pass judgement on the natural order by reference to criteria which its objective character does not establish or justify. This is what we do when we assert of a thing that it is good or evil, beautiful or ugly, true or false.

Scientists are at least as ready as any other definable group of intellectuals to accept that the human reason is capable of both this purely scientific and this "extra-scientific" function. They have no more (nor less) difficulty than the rest of us in seeing where the strictly scientific attitude is applicable and where it is not. They are as confident in applying the principle of inductive verifiability in order to reach their judgements in the laboratory as they are in forgetting the principle altogether when passing their judgements in the National Gallery. So far as this part of the argument is concerned the ground has been gone over so many times that it would be tedious to cover it again here. But outside the circles of the educated, superstitions grow apace, and the hazy, popular notion that faith normally operates in some sort of opposition to reason, seems to persist under some special diabolical protection. It is of course the peculiar blessedness of faith that it comprehends and commits itself to that which the evidence of the senses does not directly allow for. But, in spite of popular misconceptions on this point, it is certainly not a peculiar blessedness of faith that it comprehends and commits itself to that which reason can neither corroborate nor endure. E. L. Mascall has pin-pointed this particular misconception with notable clarity in *He Who Is*.

> On the other hand, there is the attitude, which has been all too common in England in recent years, according to which any real certainty in matters of religion would deprive faith of all its merit. For this school of thought, "believing where we cannot prove" becomes the essence of religion, and sometimes the suggestion is even made that God has deliberately concealed himself from us in order that we may exercise the virtue of believing on insufficient evidence. . . . [1]

The truth is that reason plays an indispensable part in formulating those credal propositions to which the man of faith commits himself. Faith rests on reason as surely as it rests on revelation and experience. Without the exercise of reason, the facts of revelation and experience could never be translated into propositions intelligible by man. The true scientist is likely to be more (not less) anxious than others to see the fullest possible exercise of reason in translating the data of divine revelation and of Christian experience into propositional form. He is likely to be more (not less) delighted than others to see the maximum precision and system in the doctrinal presentation of Christian truth.

But perhaps enough has now been said within this section to shake the reader's confidence in liberalism's claim to be speaking of the Christian Faith in a way which is peculiarly appropriate to the thinking of a scientific age. The more truly scientific our age becomes, the more justly will it weigh the claims of the dogmatist to have in Christian doctrine a rational interpretation of the meaning of existence and the purpose of the universe which can satisfy the intellect. Over against this, it must be sadly admitted that, the more semi-scholarship and illucid reflection breed

[1] E. L. Mascall, *He Who Is*, *A Study in Traditional Theism*, Longmans.

and flourish under the umbrella of inadequately disciplined subjects of study, the more we shall suffer from the fruitless interplay between pseudo-theology and ill-conceived notions of the human psyche and the human situation which at present bedevil thought in some sections of the educational world.

Is dogmatism so committed to
rational presentation of the Faith that
it violates the deeply emotional character
of man's religious experience?

Here again it can be argued that rational exploration and presentation of the Christian Faith does violence to the emotional character of Christian experience only if some antithesis is presupposed between reason and emotion. In fact, of course, such an antithesis is frequently implicit in the more careless controversial utterances of some liberal Christians. Thus one has witnessed a polemical battle recently in the theological field in which, when the case of a certain controversialist was so finely and decisively dismantled by his opponent's arguments that unconditional surrender stared him in the face, he had recourse to the claim (somewhat late in the day for so ardent a polemicist) that Christian experience, being of a profoundly emotional order, touched deeps inaccessible to the probing reason. This "argument", accompanied as it was by some of the emotive adjectives which are customarily brought into play when reason is to be denigrated (*mathematical*, *dry*, *mechanical*, etc.) is of course no argument at all. To use the machinery of rational discourse for the purpose of announcing that what you are saying cannot properly be dealt with in rational discourse is to use a particular medium of expression for the purpose of proclaiming that medium of expression to be useless. In other words it is to issue to yourself the strongest possible invitation to shut up.

Our thinking to-day is confused by the widespread assumption that reason and emotion are incompatible bedfellows, that the kind of psychological situation which produces a rational judge-ment has no connection with the kind of psychological situation which produces an emotional response. A false antithesis be-tween reason and emotion is exploited to blur many issues. Yet an emotional response, however ardent, is not necessarily irra-tional; nor is a rational judgement, however precise, necessarily devoid of emotional fervour. There is nothing irrational about brimming over with righteous indignation at the spectacle of vicious brutality. The rational man is not he who coolly sits making notes in some fatal emergency when more "emotional" men are rushing to the help of the injured. Yet popular confusion on this point leads to assumptions as outrageous as that. It would have us believe that the emotional response to the appeal of a starving beggar is to give him warmth, food, clothing, or money; while the rational response is to give him good advice or direct him to the nearest Labour Exchange. It is no exaggeration to represent popular belief thus. We have heard it voiced many a time. "Reason and emotion pull me in different directions", says the sophist, "The heart says Yes, but the head says No", when what he really means is probably, "Justice and charity commend one course, while self-interest hankers after another". It has come to this: we have heard Reason equated, not only with ratiocination unilluminated by imagination, but also with selfish and calculated pragmatism which closes its eyes to morality and charity.

An age whose literary life has been indelibly marked by the rediscovery of the poetry of John Donne and the Metaphysical poets of the seventeenth century ought surely to be the last to endure that a cloud of sentimentality should blur the true relationship between the rational and the emotional. Here per-haps is another instance of that detrimental departmentalism of our intellectual life which contributes to a general cultural dis-integration. For in this respect, as in others referred to else-where, to move from the sphere of literary studies to the sphere of journalistic thinking among the religion-discussers, is to step backward fifty years. To posit a natural antithesis between the intellectual and the emotional is, for the literary man, a mark of late nineteenth-century and early twentieth-century thinking.

A revolution has been effected in literary thinking since T. S. Eliot reacted against the musical, mellifluous, sentimental, but intellectually spineless poetry of the Georgian era. Looking for a starting-point from which to reinvigorate the languid poetic climate, Eliot found what he sought in the work of Donne. Donne's love poetry and his religious poetry both express profound emotion in intellectual equivalents so precise and vivid that the resultant blend makes an impact on the reader totally unlike the impact of most nineteenth-century poetry. As Donne recounts and explores the complex emotional experience of the lover, or of the converted sinner, he does so with a sharp intellectual analysis which is precise, economic, and busy. The immediate demand upon the reader is for an alert, clear-headed attentiveness to a packed and concentrated argument. The total effect is of encountering a brain working at white-hot intensity as the true and necessary expression of emotional fervours, conflicts, and tensions, which are too deep for the shallow flow of mere rhetoric, too strenuous to be captured by a purely musical use of imagery, too immediate to endure a vocabulary already bearing the official stamp of poetic emotivity. Eliot lamented that, after Donne, there had been a "dissociation of sensibilities" in the practice of English poetry such that this unified appeal to intellect and emotion together was lost. There is much of sharp intellectual appeal in the aphoristic, epigrammatic verse of Pope. There is much of profoundly and variedly emotional appeal in the highly sensuous and imaginative poetry of the Romantic and Victorian Ages. But, a few uninfluential exceptions apart, the central poetic tradition came to be most characteristically represented by the rich imaginative music of poetry like Keats' *Ode to Autumn*, and later by the metrical magic of Tennyson and

74

Swinburne. Valid and rich as this central poetic tradition is, it could not be denied that its fruits are only too often such as to charm the heart by putting the brain to sleep.

Now if the great literature of our country during the past forty years has a decisive character, it is precisely this, that it has integrated the intellectual with the emotional in such a way as to give to works which would cultivate the one at the expense of the other a flavour of outmodedness. This point may be verified by reference to the work of Eliot, Joyce, Pound, and David Jones, to name only four of the very greatest. In the work of each of these writers, in different ways, there is a blending of the emotional and the intellectual which constitutes a decisive, even dominant characteristic, and which also marks it as of its age. (It is notable that of these four writers one is a Roman Catholic, another an Anglo-Catholic, and a third the product of strict Jesuit education.)

In other words, culturally speaking—for the literary world at least—the expression of the deeply emotional in intellectual equivalents is itself a prime and decisive characteristic of our age. Hence the cultivation of Donne and the continuing domination of the literary scene by Eliot. Hence the drift of fashionable literary opinion against the more purely rhetorical poets like Byron and Swinburne. Hence too the drastic reassessment of the status in literary history of Shelley, Tennyson, and many of their imitators. Whatever notions may be expected to strike a note with the modern literary man, the dichotomy between intellect and emotion is not among them. Here is one more respect in which some of the pseudo-theology of the sixties belongs properly to the age of Tennyson.

In short, we belong to an age in which the cultural climate among writers and students and literature is particularly favourable to that wrestling of the intellect with the profounder claims of the spirit and with the mysteries of revelation which produces doctrinal definition. That the cultural climate of an age is favourable to a particular mode of thinking says nothing of course in itself to validate that mode of thinking. The cultural climate of an age may be a thoroughly unhealthy one. But that question is not immediately at issue here. What is immediately, and centrally, at issue is whether liberalism in theology is necessary as a means of bridging the gap between the Church and the unbelieving world; and our argument here would suggest that dogmatism in theology represents a more likely means of bridging the gap. This is partly because liberalism is apt to rely upon a concealed antithesis between the rational and the emotional which is itself invalid, and which anyway would strike the culturally awake as notably old-fashioned.

4

The Consonancy of Dogmatism

This chapter has a twofold purpose—to establish the external and the internal consonancy of Christian dogmatism. I endeavour to show that dogmatism in the theological field is in accord with valid and accredited attitudes in other fields of intellectual life. I also endeavour to show that dogmatism in the theological field is in accord with the principles operative within the Church in directing the Christian's moral and spiritual life.

It will be recognized therefore that the content of this chapter is crucial and central to the argument as a whole. But because—like everything that is fundamental in Christian thinking—it is concerned with the relationship between the temporal and the eternal, and because the eternal in itself lies outside our comprehension, the argument necessarily makes constant use of correspondence and analogy. In drawing correspondences and analogies I make frequent use of linguistic and literary illustrations. That is to say, I turn to the way language works, both in what may be called general usage, and in the more highly organized use which we call literature. Some of my reasons for choosing to refer a good deal to language and literature will be obvious: I happen to have studied in this field. But I hope too much weight will not be put on this "accident". Otherwise an important fact might be obscured—namely that this field of language and literature, and the way the human mind works in it, has a great deal to reveal to theologians and has been unjustifiably, perhaps even tragically, neglected. Further exploration of this field could surely correct some of the false recent emphases in theological thinking which have resulted from the dangerous lure held out to theologians by psychology and philosophical analysis. Indeed it would be difficult to overstress the special significance of linguistic and literary studies for the theologian. No Christian should imagine that it is possible to go far in grasping the relationship between the temporal and the eternal, in interpreting the centrality of Incarnation to the whole temporal process, without some examination of that profound biblical symbol, the Word.

We have said that the present takes its meaning, not from the future, but from the eternal. There is a supra-temporal element in all meaning. This can be seen in the nature of language itself. The word *tree* conveys a meaning for me in so far as it brings together under one head separate experiences scattered over the years in my life-story, experiences of certain growing things. The word *beauty* conveys a meaning for you and me in so far as it brings together under one head separate experiences which you and I have had over the years; experiences of features of the objective order which are far less easy to define than is a tree, but which we agree to subsume under a single term. Language, we may say, extracts from our fleeting temporal experience certain recurrent themes. It extracts them and plants them in our consciousness. By so doing, by fixing their thematic identity in a configuration which confers recognizability (for example, *justice*, as distinct from *injustice*, *influenza*, or *pin-cushion*), it creates meaning. From the moment of creation, the word (say, *justice*) rises from the dead level of the purely transient, to ride its supra-temporal course, bearing its own theme, above the reach of decay. Thus a series of threads emerges, to link together experiences past, present, and future, in your life-story and mine.

Each word I know, threading widely-spread experiences together on a single string, is a potential principle of unity around which my own past experience can be organized afresh.

The word *shoes*, if I pondered on its meaning and associations for long enough, would be capable of recovering for me all kinds of experiences from the past and knitting them together by virtue of their common point of reference. Thus a certain painful walk to school in new shoes at the age of six might link itself in the memory with a walking tour in Wales at the age of seventeen, a visit to a shoe factory in Northampton at the age of twenty, an attempt to re-sole my own shoes at the age of thirty, and a dinner party at which I wore borrowed shoes at the age of thirty-five. Any one of these scattered memories might of course be recalled in an otherwise totally different group of recollections if the operative word were not *shoes* but *school*, or *Wales*, or *factory*, or *do-it-yourself*, or *borrowed*.

A word is a potential principle of unity over-arching the passage of time. Meaning is the word in action. Meaning accrues as the word extracts the appropriate recurrent theme from your experience and mine, recovering the past, anticipating the future, involving the immediate present with them (whatever it happens to be that has triggered off the thought or use of the word here and now) in a supra-temporal configuration which unifies all it touches.

Just as language performs an organizing and unifying function by virtue of the themes which individual words configure in the human consciousness, so too the further organization of words in propositions or other logical sequences constitutes objective patterns which have a supra-temporal dimension. The statement *I love you* or *Dinner is served* has a meaning whose quality is directly related to the sheer multiplicity of widespread instances subsumed in its application. The statement *Your old friend Mr Brown is dead* reorganizes for you two rich thematic configurations (*Mr Brown* and *dead*) in a new pattern that extracts from past, present, and future so as to override all three.

The more articulate, complex, and far-reaching the organization of utterance becomes, that is to say, the more surely and profoundly patterned, the clearer will be its supra-temporal status in terms of content and in terms of construction—the greater too may be its supra-temporal status in terms of durability. To take the last point first, the collection of words which we call *Macbeth* has obviously achieved a supra-temporal status in terms of durability. But this durability would not of itself justify us in bringing the word *supra-temporal*, still less the words *timeless* or *eternal*, into use. The fact that something goes on and on does not make that thing in itself supra-temporal. The case may be quite the contrary. Only a barbarian would assert that the *timeless*, still less the *eternal* aspect of a great cathedral or a great painting or a great tragedy consists in the fact that it has survived the centuries. The concrete underground chambers of the United States Pentagon may last longer than Chartres Cathedral, but one doubts whether they will ever be cited to illustrate the "timelessness" possessed by great works of art. Indeed, the fact that something goes on and on through time may testify essentially to its sheer temporality. Such perhaps is the case with rocks.

And here we stumble upon a crucial point—a potential confusion from which our thinking has already suffered. *That which goes on and on* may be the essentially and inescapably temporal. On the other hand *that which goes on and on* may be the truly timeless or, at least, the best analogy of the eternal. A thing may go on and on through time precisely because it is of time temporal. A thing may go on and on through time because it bears the stamp of the eternal. Thus, to trespass outside our immediate subject of argument, God may be thought of in the wrong way even when we are trying to think about him in the right way. Through desperately struggling to assert God as eternal, we may succeed only in pinning him more surely and permanently within the temporal dimension. Our minds trick us. The Bishop of Woolwich is not the first to have set out to try to free God, and to have finished up by locking him in a dungeon.

Let us return to *Macbeth*, for this argument can best be con-
ducted by reference to literature, and I prefer to take a single
work that is likely to be well known to most readers, than to make
my argument unnecessarily difficult by referring to a variety of
works. The reader will appreciate that *Macbeth* is used here only
as a convenient example: the special use made of it could be made
of any comparably significant work of literature. The durability
of *Macbeth*, like the durability of any great work of art, is the
result of care lavished upon it, and that care has been lavished
precisely because the play has a genuine supra-temporal status in
terms of content and construction. Thus the durability of *Macbeth*
is an accurate expression of the play's supra-temporal meaning, just as the Church's durability through the ages is an accurate expression within the temporal order of its supra-temporal
status. *Expression* is the key word in both contexts. The Church's
supra-temporal quality does not consist in its going on and on,
but it is well expressed at the earthly level in its going on and on.
The distinction is of vital importance. If we fail to grasp it, we
may be in danger of falling into the liberal error of giving the
wrong kind of importance to the Church's temporal future. The
Church's earthly durability (it is roughly analogous to the durability of the text of *Macbeth* and to the continuing frequency of
performances of the play) is valid only because, and in so far as,
the Church has an intrinsic supra-temporal status.

Once more we must press the literary analogy. The organization of words which we call *Macbeth* is so complex and articulate,
its reference so comprehensive and yet economic, its patterning
so sure and yet extensive, that the whole has an irrefutable unity.
Harmony in diversity, lucidity in complexity, uniqueness in
distinctiveness: these "notes" are the kind of abstractions to
which we must have recourse if we would briefly characterize in
intellectual terms what, in more emotive terms, one might prefer
to call the sheer *inevitability* of the thing itself, as one, explorable,
inexhaustible, in every part and limb identifiable, or the sheer

factuality of the thing itself, as simply existing, and, once known, unforgettable, irreplaceable, inescapable. (It begins to sound like a description of God, or of the Christian Faith, or of the Church. Of course. The attempt to define what in anything bears or reveals the stamp of the eternal, whether essentially or analogously, will sooner or later begin to sound rather like a grappling towards description of God.)

There are several aspects of the "timelessness" of a work of art which can help us by analogy to understand what it means to say that the present takes its meaning from the eternal. At any given point in the experience of a poem, a tragedy, or a symphony, the full meaning is realizable only in terms of the whole. That is to say, at any given point, in listening to a Beethoven symphony, you hear a phrase which is related, in an elaborate pattern, to all that has gone before and to all that is to follow, both within the particular movement and within the symphony as a whole. The total pattern is such that the experienced listener, hearing the phrase, finds it fully enjoyable and fully understandable only in so far as the whole fabric to which it contributes is present to his mind, only in so far as he is aware of what has gone before and of what is to follow. One of the measures of the quality of a work of art will be the sureness of this inter-relatedness of all its parts. Who can listen to the third movement of Beethoven's fifth symphony without anticipating the fourth? The third movement, as we know it, is unthinkable without the fourth, unthinkable except as preceding the fourth. This logical inescapability of the total pattern, once created and experienced, may be characterized for the listener as the work's "inevitability".

In a great work of literature this aspect of the timeless is equally evident. Take a line from the middle of *Macbeth*. (I open the play at random.) "There's blood upon thy face", says Macbeth to the murderer who interrupts the banquet to report the successful despatch of Banquo and the failure to eliminate

Fleance. The better we know the play, the richer is this line's meaning for us; for the full meaning of the line can be grasped only by reference to the total pattern to which the line contributes. "There's blood upon thy face." Indeed. Our minds reach out to a score of related images, past and to come, of bloodied hands and faces and lives. On the night of Duncan's murder blood was smeared on the grooms of the bedchamber and the king's silver skin was laced with blood. There was blood too on the hands of Lady Macbeth, but not to worry, she said, a little water would soon clear her of the deed. And when we heard that claim, our minds leaped forward, sensing the irony of it. We foresaw Lady Macbeth, later on, walking in her sleep, vainly trying to clean the uncleanable hands. We had a similar experience when Macbeth announced the king's death to the young princes. "The spring, the head, the fountain of your blood/ Is stopp'd." Even as we heard that, we sensed the irony of it. We knew there was no question of a fountain of blood having been stopped. Far from it. A fountain of blood had been turned on, and neither Macbeth nor his wife was going to be able to turn it off. Already we foreheard the desperate cry, "Who would have thought the old man to have had so much blood in him?" So much blood from this unstoppable fountain that, once Macbeth stepped into the river flowing from it, he found himself so deep in blood that "returning were as tedious as go o'er". The king is killed, and it is not long before the whole country "bleeds and each new day a gash/ Is added to her wounds".

Thus the mind reaches out, backwards and forwards, from a certain point in the play. A single word, a single image, a single sentence, is enough to bring a massively rich and comprehensive fabric to mind. A fabric so rich and comprehensive that, if it were politic to do so, one could turn this book at this point into a vast exploratory survey of what *Macbeth* is about, a survey constructed around the single recurring theme of blood, thus illustrating existentially how a single line operates on the mind of Shakes-peare's reader, and making still clearer the nature of meaning itself.

We have not yet finished with the play's timelessness; for of course the universality of the play's moral and emotional applic-ability gives to the whole a supra-temporal status. And this is something more than a merely quantitative matter, something more than a question of what the logicians call "extension". That is to say, the universality of *Macbeth*, which helps to constitute the play's timelessness, is something deeper than the fact that the content of the work might carry a message fitting a multiplicity of instances, as the sentence *Dinner is served* will come in equally useful on thousands of occasions. There is much more to it than that. For the poetic overtones which rich imagery gives to a piece of literature send the mind of the reader reaching out to archetypal figures and patterns of profound and universal significance. The more systematic and organized the themes which these overtones call up, the more likely we are to use the word *symbolism* to describe the way in which they work; but of course the word *symbolic*, like the word *poetic*, refers to a quality of literature which may be present in varying degrees of intensity and in varying degrees of organization. Sometimes we recognize that the symbolic quality is so intense and systematic that we can explain the literature only by formulating it afresh—interpreting in detail. This stands for that, we say. The Prodigal Son repre-sents the Sinner returning home in penitence. His father repre-sents God. But wherever there is poetry, a symbolic element, however faint, may be present. The sensitive reader will be aware of it, though he may feel that it is so vague, or so elusive, or so fragmentary, or so delicate in its impact, that to formulate it would be to falsify it. Sometimes we murder to dissect. Never-theless, we shall miss an important aspect of the timelessness of a work of art unless we allow the archetypal symbolism of *Macbeth* to formulate itself, however tentatively. Since statements might be taken too dogmatically, let us frame the hinted-at formulation in questions.

Who is this man, tempted by ambition for the crown, by the seductive allurements of his wife, and by the preternatural promptings of the Weird Sisters, to murder his king? Who is this proud man, tempted thus by the World, the Flesh, and the Devil, to the supreme disobedience of regicide? And who is this "gracious" King, poetically surrounded by an aura of divinity, whose virtues are so many trumpet-tongued angels, who condescends to visit his subjects' home, who puts himself trustingly under his subjects' roof, who (as they admit) has given everything they have to the man and his wife, who is done to death by his own, whose murder is the great doom's image, marked by earthquake and by darkness over all the land, and of whose spilt blood one can properly say that "the wine of life is drawn"?

Thus the image of blood directs the mind, backwards and forwards within the play itself, and also to hazy significances overreaching even the play's own timelessness. "Sacrilegious murder" breaks open "the Lord's anointed temple". The "most sainted" king is murdered. His blood flows inexhaustibly through the rest of the play, life-giving wine in the veins of his faithful sons, and the indelible mark of Cain on the flesh of the unrepentant sinners.

In this argument we are concerned to explore the nature of meaning. In respect of language the nature of meaning can best be studied in poetry; for in poetry meaning can be examined with its various potentialities at their fullest stretch. Poetic imagery pushes the referential and associative functions of language to their points of maximum potency in terms of range and intensity, depth and precision. We may observe in passing that, without some degree of sensitivity to poetry, the articulation of religious thought or impulse, whether in theology or liturgy, is stultified. Not a little of the damage done by recent pseudo-theology is due to sheer inexperience of, and insensitivity to, the poetic.

We have now looked at two aspects of the timelessness of a great work of literature, quite apart from its timelessness in terms of sheer durability. We have noted that at any given point the full meaning of a given phrase is realizable only in terms of the whole. In other words, the reader who is anxious to sound the full depths of meaning that a given "moment" contains, must necessarily see "moments" from past and future gathered together with it in a supra-temporal configuration. We have also noted that aspect of timelessness constituted by the work's universality, both in terms of multiple applicability and in terms of symbolic outreach to the archetypal and the supernatural. There is a third aspect of a work's timelessness most difficult to clinch in words, yet most crucial for the purpose of our analogy.

We have already touched on this aspect when we implied that the "inevitability" caused by the sure inter-relatedness of the various elements in a great piece of literature gives to the total pattern the stamp of the eternal. That is to say, within the confines of the artistic world in which one moves when one thinks or talks about *Macbeth*, the temporal dimension of actual life, in so far as it is characterized by the cause-result sequence, complicated by the will he/won't he? question, and consequently disturbed by the powerful persistence of rejected alternatives (the might-have-beens), is not fully operative. In other words, for the reader of *Macbeth*, within the *Macbeth* world, the temporal dimension operates within the framework of a total vision which, while it never denies free-will, always allows an understanding of what is to come. Macbeth is free, yet he will fall, and we know he will fall. Here is inevitability. Yet the full inevitability of the play resides in something more than this. It resides in the fact that one cannot conceive of a *Macbeth* without the Weird Sisters. One cannot conceive of a Macbeth who never said, "My way of life is fallen into the sear, the yellow leaf". Here is inevitability—

the thing which makes it impossible for the reader to say, "If only Macbeth had taken the other road from Forres to Inverness and missed the witches", or, "If only Macbeth had said No to Lady Macbeth". Such statements in real life make sense. But a great work of art gives to the reader at every point the awareness that it could not be other than it is. The freedom experienced within the temporal remains for the characters. Yet the supra-temporal sense of the total pattern gives the reader a hindsight and a foresight which embrace this freedom within an omniscient view. So, what we meant when we said that for the reader of *Macbeth* the temporal dimension of actual life is not fully operative might be equally well (probably better) expressed by saying that the temporal dimension is *truly* operative without the limitedness which it imposes in actual life. In other words again, in experience of a great work of literature, the humanly terrestrial limitations imposed by the temporal are by-passed in such a way as to provide an excellent analogy of the difference between an intra-temporal and an extra-temporal point of view.

It is probably unnecessary to go further in arguing that a great work of literature possesses an intrinsic timelessness by virtue of the nature of its patterning, the force of its inevitability, and the universality of its reference. These qualities give the literature also the timelessness of durability. In this sense it is true that the more articulately and profoundly verbal utterance is patterned, the clearer will be its supra-temporal status in terms of content, construction, and durability.

It is time to make clear the general direction of the argument in this section. When we men attempt to "read" our world and our human situation within it, that is to say, when we try to survey our environment and take stock of our position in relationship to it, we find ourselves with two basic techniques of surveyal at our disposal—the linguistic and the mathematical. If we stretch either of these techniques to their fullest extent, we arrive at formulations which have a supra-temporal quality and which stand transcendentally arched above the phenomenal world of our immediate experience. This appears to happen in whichever direction we push a given technique of surveying the world—that is to say, if we push it beyond the stage of merely recording to the stage at which we pass a judgement or define a pattern that satisfies our hunger for "meaning". It happens, as we have just seen in the case of *Macbeth*, when the poet surveys his world, using those potentialities of language which we call "the poetic". It happens too, as I shall shortly show, when the philosopher or the moralist surveys his world, using the logical and metaphysical potentialities of language. Thus, I would argue, to exploit language to its maximum, whether in the direction of its symbolic, its metaphorical, or its rational potential, is to arrive at patterns whose meaningfulness satisfies a human demand. And these patterns, in the last analysis, have not only a supra-temporal status in terms of content and construction: they also have an objective quality which may be defined as *givenness*. Thus *Macbeth*, as well as reflecting the supra-temporal by virtue of the claims we have already made for it, also possesses a quality greater, higher, than seems explicable by reference to the ordinary human capacity and status of the individual who wrote it. We get over this difficulty by speaking of Shakespeare's *genius* or of the mystery of *inspiration*. But these terms are evasive rather than explanatory. They merely throw light on an unsolved problem: or, if you like, they give evidence of a Power from without laying his finger more markedly than is generally evident, upon a human effort to understand. Perhaps masterpieces, in the world of art, correspond more literally than we have imagined to miracles in the world of human affairs. Certainly, if we are logical, we must assign the full quality and mystery in the works of the greatest poets, artists, and composers wholly to a natural (and ultimately therefore, I suppose, investigatable and explicable) source and cause, or we must posit the co-operation of man the creator with supernatural Power in their production.

But the problem of genius is not our immediate question here. Rather I am concerned to argue, perhaps in the teeth of popular opinion, that the view which regards dogmatism in the theological field as an isolated survival of some principle which has been abandoned in every other field of knowledge and understanding, is fallacious. Indeed I would argue that in many directions in which we see man the thinker taking stock of the world and its meaning, he arrives at supra-temporal formulations which have a status and quality corresponding to the status and quality of theological dogma in the religious field, and that to reject dogma as such in the religious field would in one sense be parallel to rejecting, say, *Macbeth* in the literary field on the grounds that it never happened, or that it is too poetic, too remote from modern life, too neatly organized, too contrived, too systematic, too shot through with poetry and symbolism, too mythical, too fixed and unchanging, too unalterable, too general, too cerebral, too authoritative and magisterial, above all, too full of the mystery, the power, and the glory.

The reader must not misunderstand my analogy. I am not equating religious dogma with fiction. My argument is intended to clarify certain principles operative over the whole area in which men think and try to understand their universe and themselves. I claim that these principles operate in other fields in such a way that, if they are allowed to operate correspondingly in the religious field, they will naturally produce what we call dogma, and it may logically be expected to have an authority, status, and mystery beyond that which its human exponents would be able fully to explain or even comprehend, beyond that which could be accounted for in terms of their natural capacity. I have gone to the field of imaginative literature for my first and major illustration of this point because it is my own field, because it is a field neglected by both philosopher and theologian, and because in the theological arena especially we are beginning to see something like a division into two rival camps; which I on my side (with prejudice no doubt) would define as the camp of those aware of and sensitive to poetry and the nature of language, and the camp of those whose habit it has been (and still is) to reason without much reflection on the nature of language, and who consequently fall into naïve over-simplification of such matters as the relationship between the literal and the metaphorical. But imaginative literature is only one of several fields in which our principle can be shown to be operative. It is right to consider, though more briefly, man's linguistic exploration of his world and himself in other fields.

Man's capacity to speak is surely the first mark of his humanity, distinguishing him most notably from the animal world. It is impossible to draw a distinction between man as a *thinking* creature and man as a *speaking* creature. As C. L. Wrenn says in his book *The English Language*,

> The origin of language seems to be bound up with that of human thought. We must decide when and how man began to think, to know of the beginnings of language; and we must know when and how he began to speak, to decide on the origins of his existence as a thinking being. . . . The theory of the evolution of man as known to scientists, then, must find a place for the emergence of man as a possessor of language as distinct from the so-called "highest" species of anthropoid apes whose varied cries are not language (which implies thought), but only very fully developed conditioned reflexes . . . [1]

To mature in the use and understanding of language is to mature as a thinking creature, as a human being. For language is the chief medium of reason which distinguishes men from animals. It is the main instrument of human achievement in culture and civilization.

[1] Op. cit., p. 5.

Language, as it has developed, equips man to survey his environment in terms of qualities, substances, and processes—that is, the adjectival, the nominal, and the verbal. That language *might* have provided us, or might even yet provide us, with an equipment more precise or more appropriate to our experience than has yet been granted to us is a hypothesis which it would be fruitless to pursue at present. As it is, language, by equipping us to survey our environment in terms of quality, enables us to evaluate. It enables us to distinguish between the good and the bad, the true and the false, the beautiful and the ugly—between things which (we believe) deserve our approval and things which deserve our disapproval. By means of judgements of this kind, the things in our environment are brought into relationship with one another, organized within a system of evaluation. (A totally different system of relationships would be constructed by surveying our environment by the application of mathematical techniques, as we shall see later.)

Through language, then, we arrive at value judgements. As we become more mature in our thinking (and therefore in our linguistic sensitiveness) we begin to link our isolated value-judgements together, begin, in fact, to undertake something like a systematic reconnaissance of our universe in terms of quality. This reconnaissance, in terms of the good and the bad, the true and the false, the beautiful and the ugly (and the many gradations in between, the many qualifications and hesitancies), pushed to its limits, presents us with formulations which go some way towards satisfying an undeniable rational demand within us, and which have an authoritativeness which for working purposes we accept, while philosophically remaining sceptical of its basis. Thus our educational system, which preserves and expands our culture, is in its day-to-day work geared to an elaborate hierarchical system of values and preferences (good/bad, true/false, beautiful/ugly, etc.) which in crude or sophisticated form is brought daily into play in most fields of instruction from the nursery school to the university. Nevertheless the question "Are values absolute?", or some variant of it, is mooted at every other educational gathering or conference which is not content to look at the mere machinery of existence, but will probe in some degree the "meaning" or "purpose" of things. This contrast between practice and theory illustrates my point. Values are, in a sense, the fundamental dogma of education. We accept them. We work to them. And on the side we carry on a little intellectual game in which we pretend not yet to have made up our minds about them. (We should judge ourselves guilty of "superstition" if we openly admitted that we accept their authority in simple natural obedience.)

Note therefore what has happened in this field. By applying our linguistic technique to the surveyal of our world and ourselves in terms of quality, and therefore of value (and consequently of meaning and purpose) we have arrived at coherences (good/bad, true/false, beautiful/ugly) which (like *Macbeth*) have a supra-temporal status by virtue of their rational comprehensiveness, by virtue of their universality, and above all by virtue of that authoritativeness and mystery of theirs which the Christian will not hesitate to identify as their *givenness*. (The sceptics among us, of course, dispute the existence of the Giver. But that is another question. My argument is not directed primarily at those who dispute the existence of a Giver. Rather it is directed at the peculiar product of our superstitious age—the semi-sceptic who accepts the existence of the *Giver* but rejects almost all identifications of the *given*.)

I would not wish to restrict my argument from language to the domain of value-judgements any more than I would wish to restrict it to the domain of poetic utterance. My point can be equally well illustrated by looking at the way in which language more generally functions so as to develop and extend our organized rational and emotional life.

It is because of language that I can have certain notions and feelings about things that lie outside the confines of my limited everyday environment—about Siberia, the North Pole, Julius Caesar, the French Revolution. It is through language, used in literature, that the young learn how they ought to think and feel about things not present to them, not immediately demonstrable to them. The young learn through books what they ought to think and feel about oppression by tyrants, about courage in battle, about the exploitation of child-labour in factories and mines, the adventures of explorers, the self-sacrifice of great heroes. Thus, for the growing child and for the developing adult alike, every increase in linguistic sensitivity and awareness represents an advance in the organization of his experience. When the young child first fully grasps the meaning of the words *up* and *down*, a number of hitherto distinct experiences are newly related together. A systematic connection is established, involving, perhaps, the movement of spoon between the plate and the mouth, the position of his bedroom and the position of the kitchen, the business of toiling laboriously with the pedals of his tricycle and the far pleasanter business of letting it freewheel with the gradient. As vocabulary increases, this enrichment of the child's response to his surroundings continues apace. When he first acquires the word *suffering* with understanding, he grasps a new connection between things experienced in different ways, some of them at first hand in his own life, some of them at second-hand through books or talk—having tooth-ache, being sick, being punished, feeling lonely, dying in a desert from thirst, being knocked down by a car.

Thus every new word acquired is a point of reference around which cluster newly-related fragments of past experience, first-hand and second-hand. It is not that our words merely classify mental possessions which are already securely ours. In establishing new relationships, the new point of reference introduces us to new aspects of the architecture of the material or the immaterial universe. Perhaps the process can be seen most clearly in the acquisition of abstract terms. When I first grasp the word *concept* or the word *archetype*, the increase in my intellectual organization which results is both subjective and objective. It is subjective in that fragments of my past intellectual experience are systematized by being gathered together around a new point of reference. It is objective in that the new point of reference gives me an additional insight into the pattern of relationships which constitutes the world of ideas. And—a fact crucial to our argument—this pattern of relationships appears to have an authority independent of anything the human consciousness could endow it with. It assumes for us the status of the *discovered*, never the status of the *manufactured*.

The nature of language is such that its acquisition, and its use in constructive thinking, whether poetic or evaluative, involve us in a progress towards organization, a pursuit of order, which in the long run brings us face to face with formulations claiming a kind of supra-temporal status and authority; a status and authority which we grant for practical purposes, and even connive at "for purposes of argument", just so that our reasoning will not collapse. If we were to be honest and consistent, we should accept this pattern of our intellectual pilgrimage as symptomatic of our position in the universe, as reflecting our creaturely status, and as clearly what is to be expected in a divinely created world— namely that we should ultimately come face to face with the *givenness* of things in whichever direction the mind journeys, a *givenness* flavoured with authority and mystery.

Thus I would argue that in the various directions in which man uses his equipment as a creature of reason for the purpose of exploring his environment and himself, a point is arrived at where the equipment seems to overreach itself. Or perhaps it would be better to say that formulations are encountered which satisfy the original hunger that started man on his exploration, but whose strength and coherence cannot be wholly explained by reference to the operation of that equipment which has been used in their discovery. *Macbeth* is somehow greater than the skill of a Shakespeare can account for. Values—goodness, truth, beauty—are somehow surer than logic or philosophy can explain. The whole world of patterned relationships represented by organized abstract thinking seems to have a validity which neither semantics, nor psychology, nor science can wholeheartedly approve, and which forty years of highly-charged, intensive sceptical positivism among professional philosophers has been unable to dislodge. It is as though man's mind struggles so far towards interpretation and elucidation of the universe, and then the universe suddenly gives way, puts its own cards on the table, and suggests that man take note of them without making any more fuss.

One gathers that something approximating to this experience is known to scientists. The linguistic technique, I have said, is one of two basic equipments at our disposal for the surveyal of our world. The other is the mathematical technique which equips man to survey his environment in terms of quantity—extension, magnitude, weight, velocity. By a system of measurement we are enabled to connect together the things around us in a series of orderly relationships. Through mathematical thinking we are initiated into a mode of calculation whereby laws can be established which express the quantitative relationships between material things, and these laws enable us to classify and tabulate the operations of the natural world. The demand for order lies at the back of mathematical thinking. The significance of the isolated mathematical judgement is realized when one subsumes the judgement into a comprehensive survey of relationships which imposes order on multiplicity. "That tree is twenty-five feet high." With such a judgement we involve the tree, viewed in a certain quantitative aspect, in a systematic reconnaissance of the universe which is made in terms of number. This reconnaissance accords with our highest conception of rational consistency. It works when we apply it to practical affairs. It draws into a common pattern the minutest rhythms of the dissected atom and the massive machinery of the outer cosmos. By its manipulation we discover new harmonies and relationships wherever we extend it afresh in the realm of matter.

The pursuit of order, and the revelation of order which answers it, appear to be built-in features of man's intellectual situation. And scarcely in any other sphere than that of theology does the decadent romantic notion flourish that there is something highly questionable about this pursuit and something disreputable about the revelation which answers it. This is an ironical state of affairs, astonishing to the detached thinker, diverting to the cynic, and readily understandable only by those with an uncommonly developed awareness of the way evil works among us. Perhaps it is not too outrageous to suggest that we may be heading for a cultural situation in which a materialistic "theology" will clash head on with a highly mythological physics. However that may be, it is certain that the sentimentalized thinking which posits some *a priori* clash between a "Christianity" rooted in individual spontaneity and intellectual fog, on the one hand, and dogmatic clarity and assurance on the other hand, is pagan in origin and Pelagian in impulse.

It is time to turn from the external to the internal consonancy of theological dogmatism; that is to say, from the outer congruity of theological dogmatism with what happens in other spheres of intellectual activity in which man is brought face to face with the given, the self-authenticating, the ordered, and the rational, to the inner congruity of theological dogmatism with the principles which direct the Christian's life within the Church. There is a consistency of pattern between a Christian's development in the spiritual life, his development in the moral life, and his development in the intellectual life, which makes dogmatism as natural to orthodoxy as suspicion of dogma is natural to Pelagianism.

There is a point in the Christian's spiritual development at which he suddenly realizes that one cannot self-assertively *pray* oneself into godliness, that one can only surrender oneself to the power of the Holy Spirit. Of course one has *known* this all along, in the sense that one has been told it, has read it, has been aware of it as a statement. But there is a point at which one suddenly embraces this truth existentially and begins to try to live it. The nature of man's creaturely rôle is made plain. It is not, after all, a case of having to find God, but of allowing God to find us. Spiritual self-cultivation, in its crude and in its subtle forms, is seen for the farcical thing it is—a grotesque contradiction, laughable when it is dropped soon enough, diabolical if persisted in. We wake up to the fact that everything that matters is on offer. It is our business to receive.

The same pattern of development works itself out, of course, in our moral lives. One day the Christian wakes up to the revelation that he cannot *will* himself into virtue; that he cannot even *discipline* himself into virtue. He has tried, innocently and worthily at first perhaps, to cultivate the ideal moral self as advertised to him by schoolmasters and other exhorters of the young. But, taught by the Church, led forward by others in the Christian life, he reaches the moment when he recognizes the process of moral self-cultivation for the comic absurdity it is, and he tastes as a result something of the joy of the Christian way. He is not, after all, asked to manufacture a virtuous self to be a walking advertisement for the effectiveness of the Christian recipe for character-building. Rather he is called to obey: to accept his own creatureliness and to learn the way of submission to the commands of God and the guidance of his Spirit.

It would be odd indeed if the pattern of the Christian's intellectual development were one which violently contradicted the principles operative in the moral and spiritual spheres. But of course this is not the case. Here again the moment of truth is the moment of waking up to the real nature of the creaturely human rôle, waking up to the realization that one does not have to construct a set of beliefs or search vainly for them through the mists of doubt, but to receive a faith revealed, explained—infinitely explorable, yes, certainly—but *there*, on offer. The joy of this realization is the joy of conversion, the joy of seeing that God who planted the body's hunger provides the food that satisfies it, that God who planted the soul's hunger provides the food which satisfies it, that God who planted the intellect's hunger provides the food which satisfies it. He gives the hunger and the food, the appetite and the satisfaction, the search and the end. But of course one has to learn to *receive*, to forget the self's niggling determination to do things independently, off its own bat. One has to learn to get beyond the self's persistent self-assertiveness in the self-aggrandizement of acquisition whether it be in the spiritual, in the moral, or in the intellectual sphere. In the Christian life nothing, nothing at all can be purchased at the do-it-yourself shop.

Theological dogmatism is fully consonant with the Christian view of the human situation and with the Christian view of God. Man's creaturely status being what it is, his dependence upon the Creator being what it is, and God's love for his creatures being what it is, we should expect God to provide that which answers all the needs he has implanted in man. We should expect these answers to be of such a kind that they will be adequate to man in his situation in time and yet *not* of such a compulsive, irresistible character that man's freedom is destroyed. Compulsive, irresistible dogmas, manifestly irrefutable, would take away man's freedom. If the doctrines of the Trinity, the Redemption, and the Incarnation were so rationally self-evident or so plausibly verifiable that no developed human mind, having once encountered them, could reject them, then God would not in this respect have provided answers to man's needs, rather he would have wiped out the needs. In short, there must be the gap between the human brain and religious truth which preserves man's freedom; but, the gap having been bridged by the individual, the truth itself must *be* the truth: otherwise man is tricked.

The mistake of liberalism is that it tries to preserve man's freedom by tampering with the nature of truth, as at present attainable, by questioning its authority at this stage. At the same time liberalism tries to deny the existence of the gap between the human brain and religious truth. The ironical result of this is that if Christian truth were what the liberal assumes it to be—something as yet unverified but eventually to be fully authenticated by the same procedures as those by which one gathers more information about the phenomena around us, then (assuming that the pursuit of truth is itself worth while) there would come a time (a *time*, I say) when Christian truth would have been authenticated in such a way that man's freedom would be destroyed. The hidden presumptions of liberalism are as audacious as that. Liberalism's rejection of the human status is indeed as old as Adam and Eve. The voice of theological liberalism first spoke in the garden. "There is no gap, no mystery, no veto. The fruit of the tree is yours for the taking. Ye shall be as gods. It is only a question of time."

It is important to understand how theological liberalism obliterates human freedom, for the operation is an undercover one, effected in the same manner as a conjuring trick. The gap between the human brain and the formulation of revealed truth is the guarantee of man's freedom at the intellectual level. Man is free to leap the gap and embrace the truth or to remain on this side in ignorance. By presupposing a Christian truth authenticable by the inquiring mind in a stage-by-stage process of discovery and verification, liberalism virtually abolishes the gap which constitutes the guarantee of man's freedom. This abolition of freedom is concealed because its effects are *postponed* to a future date—the time when the authentication of Christian truth (which the liberal pursuit itself presupposes) will be complete. But the abolition of freedom is no less real for the fact that it is not going to be commonly noticed yet. The abolition of freedom *in time* is just as sure a rejection of the human status when the

99

abolition is located in the future as it would be if the abolition were located in the past.

That theological liberalism should attract political "progressives" who assume the perfectibility of man and anticipate the establishment in time of a wholly satisfying, just, and happy social order, is natural. All heresies in the long run derive from the same root, the same rejection of the creaturely human status. This rejection involves saying No to freedom, to dependence, and to suffering.

If man says Yes to freedom and to dependence, and says Yes equally to the concept of a God of Love, he thereby insists that man has needs, that God answers them, and that his answers do not make man any less free. On this basis, there will be a theological dogma of such a kind that it can satisfy the inquiring mind of the intellectual and, at the same time, can be so expressed as to feed the mind of the simple and the uneducated. It will be complete. It will *offer* such satisfaction as is appropriate for the creature in time. It will demand the leap of faith which is needed in all departments of Christian experience, in all movements of the Christian life. Once the leap has been made, what is embraced will prove rich, full, rewarding, more than enough—but *never* compulsive after the fashion of compulsions which eradicate freedom and deny love.

We cannot remove the necessity for the leap by denying the gap without destroying human freedom. We cannot question the fullness and adequacy of the truth that is leaped to, without throwing doubt on God's love. But this *fullness* and *adequacy* are the properties of food which nourishes, not of drugs which destroy, the appetite. (The liberal theologian's picture of orthodox doctrines as intellectual slimming pills which atrophy the mind's appetites, and whose side-effects include a loss of cerebral virility, will not stand up to scrutiny.) After the grappling and hesitation comes the leap: and after the leap the moment of fulfilment—and fulfilment is always acceptance. This is the pattern of the Christian way: for of course it is the pattern of the human way. The moment of truth is always a moment of acceptance, never a moment of mastery. Unless we recognize the intellectual as well as the moral and spiritual implications of this principle, we shall continue to suffer from that sickness which erodes our religious life—that schizophrenia by which we try to train ourselves to crawl in creaturely submission as moral and spiritual beings, while we pose as gods in the world of the intellect. God is a better craftsman that we would allow him to be. He has made us all of a piece. The principles of his way with his children which we learn (or fail to learn) so laboriously through the discipline of prayer and of the moral life are principles applicable to our situation in all fields of activity, the intellectual field included. God *gives*. We are always wanting self-assertively to make, to do, to get there of our own initiative, under our own steam, by-passing the *givenness* of all that matters importantly to us. Of course we have to work, to strive, to study—but all the working and striving and studying in the long run bring us face to face with the *givenness* of the nourishment by which body and soul and mind are fed.

Here it is. This is it. It has been waiting for me all along. Such are the responses characteristic of the Christian moment of fulfilment: not—*Now I've done it. At last I've got there. Thank God, I've hammered out the truth at last.* But then is not this true of all our experience in striving towards what seems worth having, worth loving, worth enjoying, worth knowing? Why should we expect the pattern of progress towards knowledge and understanding of God's truth to be different from all other patterns of progress towards what satisfies, fulfils, illuminates, or nourishes the human heart, the human brain?

Let us follow up another analogy.

Some years ago James Kirkup, the poet, gave a talk on the radio about the composition of his poem *A Correct Compassion*. Kirkup described how he had been allowed to be present in the operating theatre to observe a major surgical operation. The experience was naturally a moving one, and he was anxious to sum it up in poetic form. But he did not rush away to write it up as a journalist would have done. Rather he waited, struggling with words and lines for several weeks, gradually allowing the poem to take its own shape. When it was finished, then, he told us, he was able to say, "Yes, *that* is what the experience was like".

In short, the formulation in poetry was needed before the experience itself could be fully known for what it was. This is in keeping with the nature of poetry, indeed with the nature of linguistic utterance. I take it that, James Kirkup having reached that point, having organized and thereby *recognized* his own experience thus, his next experience of an operation, if he has another, will be different, richer, from the fact that the poem was written and the previous experience organized. That is to say, artistic formulation of experience enriches the experience it formulates and stabilizes it for the future. If you write a poem about the sea, your future experience of the sea will not be quite the same as if you had not written it. This principle is of course important in the field of education. If a child writes freely and creatively about the countryside, two things happen. In the first place fragmentary past experience of the countryside is organized and fully recognized. In the second place future experience of the countryside is enriched.

What applies to the writing of poetry applies conversely to reading too. This is one of the things which distinguishes poetry from journalism. (By "poetry" here I mean imaginative literature whether in verse or in prose.) If I read a poem about the sea, some fragments of my past experience of the sea are organized in such a way that the moment of *recognition* dawns upon me. "Yes, of course, *that* is what the sea was really like!" Correspondingly my future experience of the sea is enriched. For the poetic formulation has brought me a clarification, indeed a *realization*, of what my own past experience of the sea really amounted to. In the light of this realization, I return to the sea next time with a fuller and richer awareness of what human experience of the sea amounts to.

The analogy—the parable, if you like—which this account of literary experience provides for what happens when the Christian explores humbly the whole field of authentic traditional doctrinal utterance, is too obvious to be pressed home point by point. But one aspect of the parallel deserves to be lingered upon—namely, the fact that the pattern of development, as just described, applies not only to poetry which is easily assimilable and superficially attractive. Indeed it is profoundly true of some of the most formidable—superficially most forbidding—literature we encounter. The corresponding implications of this fact in the theological field ought not to be overlooked.

Consider the matter in the literary field first. The teacher, introducing a group of students to something "difficult"—say Eliot's *The Waste Land*—may find among his pupils a young "rebel" who puts his teacher into exactly the same position as the teacher who is trying to persuade the sceptical young that, say, the doctrine of the Trinity, is worth thinking about. The young rebel, the literary "layman", the straightforward and no-nonsense fellow who means business, faces *The Waste Land* and recognizes a formulation so formidable that he turns away in honest impatience. The enthusiast for poetry tries to persuade, to explain. The literary "layman" will have nothing to do with it. "The more you explain, the more you put me off. All your talk only goes to show that this is an elaborate intellectual game played by a group of people who are out of touch with real life, remote from the hard, vital facts of existence. True poetry must be simple and appeal directly to the heart. It must directly convey the deep emotional responses of plain men and women involved in the ordinary affairs of daily life. It must touch their hearts and minds, evoking a sure sympathetic response. It must have the immediate self-authenticating notes of spontaneity and sincerity. The ramifications of intellectual abstruseness of this kind can never express any warm, living truth. The need to explain allusions and references and far-reaching implications gives the whole game away. It is all too intellectual, too dry, complex, remote from modern life . . ."

Where have we heard these accents before if not from those who object against formulations in another field—namely, the theological?

Do we give in? In the literary field, do we give in? Do we hang our heads and say, "Yes, I suppose you're right. Man has come of age. He is ready now for poetryless verse"?

The teacher of literature has perhaps an easier task than the teacher of theology. The powers-that-be in the literary world have not sold the pass behind his back. He explains that, with every reading of *The Waste Land*, once the initial surrender to its "authority" as poetry has been made, the mind will respond more and more eagerly until it is saying of each formulated utterance that the poem contains, "Yes, that's it". With every passage of the poem another penetrating experience of our civilization is organized and expressed in such a way that we receive an illuminating recovery and recognition of our own profoundest responses to the world we live in. Through submission to the poem's authority, and through mental effort in exploring its deep and far-reaching content, we find our own experience of our civilization at last recognizably articulated, and we return to share in the life of that civilization with a much surer, more sensitive, and more penetrating awareness of its nature.

Theological dogma makes to the Christian an offer of comparable character. The Christian is invited to explore a formulation of truth which is perhaps superficially forbidding, certainly formidable. At first, perhaps, it repels by its massiveness, its "irritating" sureness, its precision, its dryness. One kicks against what appears to be an over-intellectual mode of utterance, lacking the immediate appeal to the emotions which the easy, blurred, and evasive slogans of consolatory liberalism put before us. Just as there is a lax indolence within us which, if indulged, would enable us to be content with cheap verse, oozing with maudlin sentimentality, tricked out with every alluring quality—the mellifluous, the pretty, the highly-coloured, so too there is an intellectual indiscipline and a spiritual laziness within us which would prefer the cosy nebulosities of pseudo-theology to the crisp clarities of dogma that requires to be grappled with before it yields its full fruit.

The grappling, if it is reverent and not self-assertive, if it is honest and not ulteriorly motivated, leads to acceptation. On page after page, as the faith is expounded and explored by the orthodox writer, the reader meets the formulation which makes him say, "Yes, that's it". He responds to each further revealing of a traditional doctrine's implications with the delighted "Of course!" Every additional illumination is as of something one knew all the time, yet never fully faced and recognized before. One is increasingly aware of moving in a world that is both incessantly exciting, and yet warmly familiar. How can one express its "excitingness" without uncharity—without confessing that, after feeding on solid doctrinal orthodoxy, the speculations of liberalism are just plain *boring*; boring in that they present the vitally Christian mind with acres and acres of what one can in honesty only call tediousness? As for the warm familiarity of doctrinal orthodoxy, it amounts to this. Reading, one is forever encountering men and women whose experiences have matched, or balanced, or contrasted with one's own in such a way that their "discoveries" answer one's own needs, solve one's own problems. Gradually the very quality, the flavour, the tang, the atmosphere of their world impresses itself on the mind as the genuinely "Christian". (Then, perhaps, one has to resolve for oneself the difficult problem of finding the right word to describe that other world of pseudo-theology into which the Christian "tang" so rarely intrudes.) It is the "Christian" by virtue of two thousand years of human agreement under divine corroboration, and no ephemeral aberration of a decade, or even a century, can weaken the identification. An outbreak of unbelief among a group of professional theologians in the nineteen-sixties is as powerless to weaken this lasting identifiability of the truly *Christian* as all such outbreaks have proved in the past. (One must not exaggerate the damage that such outbreaks do. Professional theologians, and even clergy, have been in all ages especially prone to loss of faith. By the very nature, both of theology and professionalism, the temptation to loss of faith is likely to come in especially dangerous form to men of such calling, in whose minds the demand to bring light and help to others readily assumes the insidious character of a *personal* and *individual* responsibility such as no Christian is in fact asked to carry, and such as destroys the creaturely sense of dependence within the Church upon its inherited wisdom. The modern intellectual climate in which our professional theologians and other ecclesiastics freely and honestly admit their loss of faith has great advantages over a climate in which hypocrisy and pretence would be encouraged.)

If you pick up a book in the study of an orthodox Christian reader, you will see what I mean. As you turn the pages, you come upon sentences which have caused the reader to take out his pencil, to underline the text, to place excited ticks in the margin. Study the sentences in question, and ten to one you will find that they represent points at which the immediate, contemporary, and personal reference of some traditional doctrine has been finely formulated—formulated, that is, so as to awaken in the reader that recovery and recognition of his own experience which demonstrates the universal applicability of the doctrine in question.

He would be a foolish man who imagined that moments of glad acceptance, such as these, could occur only to the reader of easy, indisciplined, and strongly emotive literature, whether theological or imaginative. Indeed, the student of literature who goes far in his subject learns that the greatest treasure often lies hidden. There is often a hard shell of apparent formidability, obscurity, or elusiveness to crack before the kernel can be savoured. How long has it taken even the "highbrows" to realize that much the finest work of literature to come out of the 1914–18 war is David Jones' *In Parenthesis*? How long will it be before this realization has got through, as it surely must, to the general reader?

The experienced reader of literature is of course neither surprised nor much disturbed by paradoxes such as this. He recognizes that Kafka, say, was unread in his own day for much the same reason that Kierkegaard, say, was comparatively unread in his. There are paradoxes of other kinds too. We are no more surprised at what some of to-day's academic theologians say about C. S. Lewis, for example, than we are surprised to read what their ancestors had to say about Kierkegaard. We are not even surprised, some of us, to see Kierkegaard quoted and cited in support of (or as ancestor of) the liberal theology of our own age which, as any careful reader of Kierkegaard must know, he would from the very depths of his being have abhorred.

Enough of paradoxes. Probably Kafka will provide me with the best analogy to press my point about the contrast between the "shell" and the "kernel". For Kafka is a writer superficially empty of relevance, at first sight involving the reader in a world of fantasy remote from the actualities of twentieth-century daily life. But how false all superficial and "first-sight" reactions to Kafka turn out to be for the reader who submits to the authority of Kafka's "poetic" idiom and takes the intellectual trouble to explore his allegedly "unreal" world.

How unreal does that world turn out to be, when we put it alongside the plainly naturalistic world of, say, E. M. Forster's *Howard's End*? (In order to be fair, I choose a first-rate writer in the naturalistic tradition for purposes of pressing home my contrast, and therefore no denigration of Forster is intended.) The answer, in my particular case, is that my daily experience takes me back in mind frequently to Kafka, rarely to Forster. This may be partly because I work in the educational world. At any rate, there is scarcely a day on which the ticking over of the educational machinery, the drifts of discussion, the movements of thought and action, the operations of meetings and committees, the recommendations of the Ministry of Education and other "authorities", do not reinforce the conviction that careful reading of Kafka's *The Castle* long ago established in me—"This is the real world. This is the world I know. This is the world I have always worked in. Here it is, the thing itself, explicated as surely as any literary utterance could hope to do it." And this response, evoked so frequently by one's working life, is equally in tune with much that one daily lives through in the personal field, in the field of authorship, and even in one's specifically religious life. And yet how forbidding, austere, metallic, unreal, the world of *The Castle* on first acquaintance is likely to seem.

Enough is enough. The point has been made. If the arguments used against the rigorously doctrinal in the theological field were to be paralleled in the literary field, the most profound and significant formulations of human experience in imaginative literature would be denigrated, neglected, and eventually, I suppose, lost to the world.

5

The Relativity of the
Human Viewpoint

The departmentalism of modern thinking has made many of us schizophrenic. Owen Barfield, in his stimulating book, *Saving the Appearances*, has explored an important instance of our schizophrenia. He points to what we have learned from physicists in recent years about the close interdependence of the phenomenal world as presented to us through our senses and the nature of our own consciousness. This interdependence is such that we must perhaps reckon with the phenomenal world that confronts our common sense as largely a construct of our own consciousness. We must certainly take into account the vast discrepancy between the physicist's description of the construction of, say, a piece of furniture, and the description of the same piece that accords with our familiar experience of it. On the one hand the physicist displays mathematical formulae and inflated nuclear "models" that look like networks of sticks or clusters of billiard balls, and tells us that these fairly represent the real basis of the material things about us. On the other hand perception conveys to our consciousness a series of constructs that have firm outline and colour known through sight, texture and solidity known through touch. We may utilize this now generally accepted discrepancy between the strict scientific account of the world and the common-sense account either for the purpose of depreciating the reliability of science or for the purpose of decrying the reliability of common sense. We may argue that the world known to science is a "mere abstraction", or that the world known to common sense is a "mere construction" of our own consciousness. In either case we press home the discrepancy. There is no reconciliation. The interdependability of the world of familiar objects and the nature of our own consciousness is established.

Nevertheless, as Barfield brilliantly illustrates, this principle of interdependability, with all its enormous implications, is thrown overboard when we turn from physics or psychology to the study of pre-history or geology. We accept in these spheres, without question, that the world as known to human consciousness is capable of being studied and described throughout ages of time in which there was no human consciousness to know it. (We also accept, I might add, that time, as we reckon it, "functions" according to that system of reckoning even if there are no human beings to reckon it.) In other words, the human consciousness, fully developed as it is, has had a few thousand years of interdependent life with a world which it has learned to "know" and to describe in terms appropriate to the peculiar mode of that interdependence. And on that basis we have posited a world behaving in a fashion corresponding to those terms over millions of years during which there was no interdependence with human consciousness to give those terms any kind of relevance, applicability, or meaning. We have for several hundred years, in the sciences and the arts alike, studied our environment, developing certain measuring rods for this purpose. But we do not know how far the very environment we have studied and the measuring rods we have used owe their apparent character to the peculiarities of our own consciousness, or indeed to the nature of that interdependence between our consciousness and our world by virtue of which the confrontation between subject and object takes the form it does. Certainly we have need to be sceptical about the final validity of flinging our little measuring rods about over vast reaches of space or time (as they appear to us) that are freed from any interdependence with human consciousness.

Those familiar with the work of R. G. Collingwood will recall some of the warnings he wisely gave us in this connection. One of the illustrations he used is so lively as to be worth repeating. Granted the molecular structure of our world as understood by modern physics, there would appear to be a *minimum space* within which any substance can exist as such. That is, to put it crudely, if water is made up of two parts hydrogen to one part oxygen, there must be a minimum quantity of water such that if this minute droplet were further "cut", one would be left with hydrogen on the one side and oxygen on the other. Or, to put it another way, there must be a minimum space within which water can be water: if that space is contracted water ceases to be water and becomes something else—hydrogen or oxygen. (Of course this argument is not meant to be taken as an account of a possible experiment, but rather as an exploration of the logical implications of current scientific exposition.) It follows that one can conceive, theoretically speaking, of a creature whose eyesight is so microscopically sharp and so minutely focused that when he looks at what we know as water he will see something else. On the basis of this argument one can bring into question the general applicability of our particular "span of perception" in the spatial field—an applicability which both science and common sense tend to regard as universal and final.

Comparable to the notion of *minimum space* is that of *minimum time*. Again granted the molecular structure of our world as described by modern physics, it is plain that matter exists at the basic level of the particle by virtue of certain movements and relationships set up between proton and electrons within the nucleus. The analogy of the dance is sometimes used to give the mind a model by which the process can be grasped. It must be accepted that the movements within the atomic nucleus which lies at the base of matter take place within time. In short, it would seem to follow that there must be a minimum time within which electrons can move around the proton sufficiently to establish the pattern which constitutes the particle. That is, to simplify crudely, there must be a minutely brief section of time such that, if it were further "cut" in two, there would be insufficient time for a particle of hydrogen to establish itself as such. The necessary movements could not take place. Thus we can conceive, theoretically, of a creature capable of giving a glance so quick, so brief, at a material object that the object would not have time to construct itself. Where we see a door, this hypothetical creature would see "nothing".

Now, that these arguments are perhaps only of analogical significance does not, I think, affect their usefulness for our purpose. They represent a mode of reasoning which would constitute in any practically conceivable situation that science is at present likely to contrive for us, a valid questioning of the applicability of what Collingwood calls our "spans of perception" over areas of space and time so vast that the mind surrenders its grasp in trying to contemplate them. Above all, they emphasize, like Barfield's argument, that peculiar *fittedness* of our machinery of perception and consciousness to the world on which it operates, or, to put it in a better way, to that basis with which that machinery co-operates so as to construct what we know as our familiar environment.

What kind of view of life we hold will be determined by the kind of data we accept as being characteristically representative of the universe we inhabit and the state of being in which we share. That is to say, our philosophy will be one which accords with the pattern of things as suggested by those particular events and aspects of our experience which seem to us expressive of the true underlying character of the totality compounded of our world and ourselves. If we are selective and arbitrary in singling out aspects of our experience which are made to carry the weight of a generally applicable significance, we shall necessarily acquire an unbalanced view of what life is all about. Correspondingly, if we accustom ourselves to the schizophrenic practice of ignoring what we have learned in one realm of experience when turning our attention to another, we shall never arrive at an overall philosophy, or at best arrive at a distorted one.

It is observable that an obsession with machinery of any kind tends to produce a bias towards mechanistic thinking outside the strict sphere of its applicability. The century which has seen the most rapid advances in the invention and use of machinery has also exhibited the drift towards mechanistic thinking with reference to such matters as human psychology, human relationships, the nature of human society, and even with reference to the purpose and functioning of the universe. Similarly, an obsession with the plant world and the animal world tends to produce a bias towards evolutionary thinking—thinking in terms of blind growth and development—in reference to such matters as the mind of man, the nature of education, the history of civilizations, or the overall destiny of the universe.

Thus far in the argument, one might say, I have been concerned with twin caveats against the parallel and converse dangers of schizophrenia and selectivism. Schizophrenia tempts us to shed what we have learned in one sphere of experience when we turn to another. Selectivism tempts us to erect the underlying principles discerned in one given area of experience into principles of universal application to the whole that life presents us with. It goes without saying that unconscious selectivism on the basis of principles discerned in one or two fields of science and technology (not physics) has been the main threat to our cultural, educational, philosophical, and religious thinking this last hundred years. It is fortunate, perhaps, that competing selectivisms tend to cancel one another out; though the spectacle of the competition naturally gives rise to a despairing awareness of a culture without rudder, a civilization that has lost its intellectual bearings. And finally, as a by-product of the philosophy-less society, comes the denigration of philosophy itself.

Of course, unlike instances of schizophrenia, instances of selectivism, especially of conscious selectivism, may do much good in correcting already powerful biases. It may be argued that Owen Barfield's own thesis in *Saving the Appearances* represents a case of selectivism. It is none the less valuable as a corrective. Barfield's selection of the experience of a rainbow, and his use of the experience as an analogy to characterize the relationship between human consciousness and the human environment is wholly illuminating. The example transforms the reader's estimate of the objective reliability of the world as it confronts common sense, and compels him to ask how far the human consciousness generally co-operates in constructing the phenomenal world, after the fashion in which it co-operates in constructing the rainbow. One surely has as much right to take one phenomenon as another and to judge our experience of it to be analogically significant, capable by correspondence of enriching our understanding of other experience. Or has one? Are there grounds for, say, preferring our experience of a desk as a more reliable basis for philosophical generalization than our experience of a rainbow? Does the fact that we can touch the desk as well as see it render the experience a more reliable basis for argument about the nature of the phenomenal world and our relationship to it? And, if so, is this because the sense of touch takes precedence over the sense of sight? Or is it merely that the evidence of two senses is surer than the evidence of one?

We do, in fact, I think, generalize our experience into judgements on the basis of a hierarchical system of precedence, in respect of the reliability of the senses, which is perhaps not easy to defend. We feel "surer" of things which we can touch as well as see, of things we can see as well as hear. And yet this system of precedences, valid as it may be for our situation as it is, is perhaps, together with that "situation" itself, the product of a relationship between man and his environment which might have developed in a totally different way.

This point can be satisfactorily made only by illustration which is hypothetical and highly fanciful. Man is such that, within limits, he *chooses* what he shall see—by opening or closing his eyes, by looking this way or that. But he cannot, in the same way, choose what he shall hear. That is chosen for him. He cannot open or close his ears at will. On the other hand, so long as his senses are active (he is not asleep, his eyes are open, his ears are unplugged) he is seeing things all the time, but he is hearing things only intermittently. If I am in the room with you I do not have to make any effort in order to be seen by you, but I have to make an effort in order to be heard by you.

I wish to suggest that the situation might conceivably have been the reverse of this. The history of the universe and the human race might have been such that we should now hear sounds all the time except when we voluntarily close our ears to give ourselves a rest or go to sleep. Imagine that we could choose what to hear or what not to hear by our control of our earflaps and by turning our heads this way and that, in a world as permanently full of sounds as our world is permanently full of "sights". Imagine too that, even though our eyesight is not "defective", we do not see anything at all (the equivalent of silence), except when something inserts itself forcefully into our field of vision (the equivalent of making a noise). Thus, if you were in the room with me I should be hearing you all the time. You could not help that. Indeed your sound, your music, would be the sign of your presence. You would have a persistent audible musical construction instead of a stable visual one. This involuntary music would be your "appearance", your known outside by which you would be recognized. As one gets near you, you get louder, so that collisions are avoided. On the other hand you are not consistently visible. You are invisible except when you make a conscious effort to be seen by others. You communicate with others by thus consciously and with effort inserting yourself into their field of vision. You are able to do this in a variety of shapes: it requires an effort: the technique has to be learned: this technique is the "language" of men and women. And just as the audible language of the tongue in our world as it is can be transferred on to paper so that the eyes can read it in silence, so in this world of fancy the picture language of self-shaping can be transferred in audible symbols to a kind of tape-recorder which enables us to "read" your works when so inclined.

Is it too fanciful to suggest that the secret of the appeal of music lies in the fact that it introduces us to the world we *might* have been living in, had evolution taken a different turn, had the ear and hearing developed a priority over the eye and seeing? Is it too fanciful to suggest that the secret of the appeal of art lies in the fact that it introduces us to the world we *might* have been living in, had the language of communication been an essentially visual medium based on the wilful insertion of the personality into another's field of vision in a series of ever-changing shapes and colours—an utterance emanating from a permanently audible but predominantly unseen "base"?

Speculations of this kind should accord well with the spirit of an age which has seen such remarkable progress in the transmission of both sound and spectacle over vast distances. And they constitute a healthy reminder of the limited and perhaps (taking a cosmic view) very odd, very unbalanced, very peripheral stance which our equipment of sense and consciousness gives us and from which we must survey our world.

The purpose of this fanciful hypothesis, as of the argument in general in this section, is to encourage scepticism about the reliability of that framework of assumptions within which what is usually called "scepticism" (*vis-à-vis* religion, for instance) operates. In particular I posit a might-have-been world in which men and women are always, by their very presence in it, emitting sound waves to other men and women, whose equipment for receiving them is always active (except when voluntarily shut off) and whose consciousness is fed by an elaborately differentiated code of interpreting these emissions, so that the whole business of making sounds and receiving them operates with the priority and significance with which, in our actual world, the business of being visible and being looked at operates. Likewise I posit a world in which men and women make themselves visible only by a special voluntary effort. To become visible is to effect a disturbance in the visual field which is registered involuntarily by those who are within "eyeshot". (The eyes need no covers. They do not open or shut. Their covers are as rudimentary as our existing ear-flaps.) The nature of this disturbance, by which we wilfully insert ourselves into another's field of vision, is such that shape and colour and movement are involved in a highly organized and articulated system of signs and "compositions". This is our language, our means of communication. Modern painters perhaps give us some idea of what such a means of communication might be like. Perhaps we taste the delight of using what is at the present evolutionary point an undeveloped means of expression and communication when we enjoy modern art. In the same way, when we enjoy music, we savour the nature of a might-have-been existence consequent upon an evolutionary development which did not happen, moving about in a world not realized, a world whose total architecture of person and object, woof and fabric, is audible rather than visible.

My excursion into hypothesis will not have been fruitful unless it has laid bare the fact that, in the world as it is, we accept a system of precedences and priorities which is inescapably tied to a mode of consciousness strongly directed by the fact that some of our senses have developed more than others. We "trust" a thing more if we can see it than if we can only hear it. We "trust" a thing more if we can feel it than if we can only see it. (Barfield's rainbow, for instance.) We accord a degree of reality to the chair which we do not allow to the rainbow. To such an extent have we allowed a concealed bias in favour of the sense of touch to colour our thinking that our vocabulary of reliability is rich in metaphors of solidity. I want *tangible* proof, we say. Here is *solid* evidence. This is an *unshakeable* case. In the last resort, when we are defending what we consider to be essential truth, we are not content with metaphors drawn from the process of seeing. To argue that a case is *clear, lucid, illuminating, vivid, bright, dazzling*, may be to give high praise to the case for its power to interest or to entertain. But to argue that a case is *solid, tough, rocklike, unshakeable*, is to give the maximum testimony to its truth and reliability.

Thus, I argue that our thinking generally operates on the basis of a concealed preference in reliability granted to the sense of touch at a time when physicists have themselves knocked the bottom out of any theory of matter on which such a precedence could reasonably be based. In the same way I argue that we accept a system of precedences in relation to the relative reliability of touch, sight, and hearing, in that order, which, in so far as it is appropriate (and the scientists are making us wonder whether it really is), is appropriate only as expressing a particular and complex relationship between man and his world which, far from being absolute and logically necessary, can easily be unthought by anyone who takes the trouble to unthink it.

In short, the interdependence of human consciousness and universe, as "known" through sensation and perception, is such as to bring into question the applicability of human measuring rods outside the limited boundaries within which that interdependence is clearly established. Secondly, the mode of knowing characteristic of this state of interdependence between human consciousness and "known" universe, has had its priorities determined by the delicately balanced development of man's various senses which happens to have taken place. Philosophically speaking, it need not have happened like that. That is to say, science itself gives us good reason to suspect that reality is of such a kind that a quite different balance in the development of the respective senses *might* have obtained, giving a very different character to the interdependence between human consciousness and known universe, and to the mode of knowing which articulates it.

When one adds to the potential unreliabilities here discerned at the basis of our knowledge the previously mentioned unreliabilities due to the fallibility of human judgement and represented by the twin tendencies to "schizophrenia" and to "selectivism", one has accumulated a formidable battery of second-degree scepticism with which to assail that first-degree scepticism on which so much contemporary superstition is erected and which undergirds pseudo-theology.

One of the misfortunes of our present intellectual situation is, I believe, that over the last half century a heavily biased, but unconscious selectivism has operated to establish a notion of "manhood" which is neither deductively nor inductively defensible. That is to say we have an unexamined presupposition about what may be justly posited as the human "norm" or "standard man" at the starting-point of philosophical or religious argument. We tend to start our thinking from a tacitly accepted concept of "basic man" in relation to whom, for instance, any rich artistic, imaginative, or mystical experience would be peripheral and eccentric. "Basic man" is the product of a concealed bias bred of unconscious selectivism. Since we wish to reason only on the surest possible foundations, and since our built-in hierarchical system of sense-preferences relates sureness to tangible three-dimensional solidity, we posit mentally, as "basic man", a boxed-up consciousness whose prime function is to compete for space with chairs and tables. What kind of a consciousness this is and whether it fully gets into touch with other consciousnesses are questions we defer until surer matters have been explored. And surest among the sure matters seems to be the fact that on the surface of this planet solid bodies are jostling one another, ourselves among them. This would be well and good, were it not that science has now deprived us of objective solidities and substituted a network of dancing electrons. The atomic ballet seems to be here to stay for some time, and it has knocked the bottom out of naïve materialism.

I would suggest that conscious selectivism (in itself as justifiable as any unconscious selectivism) might offer us a new "basic man" whose relationship to the world would be such that we should have to rethink a lot of our prejudices. Suppose, for instance, we were to start with sexual man, or man the Nature mystic, or man the artist? Does the rich and varied responsiveness that man reveals in his sexual life show him in an uncharacteristic light? Or is it perhaps proper to man's true nature that he should exhibit something like this variety and intensity of responsiveness in relation to a far wider range of experiences than the sexual? We have the evidence of the poets and mystics of Nature that man's responsiveness to the world of hills and valleys, trees and flowers, sky and sea, can exhibit a comparable scale of gradations from the prosaic to the sublime. Again, there is much in impressionist painting to suggest that men with open eyes and lively imaginations can enter with a mood of divination and of joy into the contemplation of things so prosaic and superficially unattractive as a dirty city street scene on a foggy winter night or a bare kitchen table and chair in an apparently drab garret. Might it be that man could be moving about a world offering an endless and diverse series of illuminations to delight and stir the emotions if his true potentials were brought into play? Might it be that man would be most surely himself if his daily encounters with the simple objects around him sparked off the responsiveness now assumed appropriate only to romantic young lovers, genius-ridden artists, and gifted poets, and to them even only fitfully?

It seems to me that we have decided in advance in favour of a "basic man" in relationship to whom any very rich experience is eccentric. One detects in the prevailing climate of opinion a preference for the space-occupying feeding and computing machine as the most reliable human image to serve as a basis when *starting* an argument about the nature of man, the only possible universal presupposition, the highest common factor of irrefutability. Even Christians themselves do not escape the infection of this prejudice. We are continually reminding ourselves, through sermons and books, that in any true estimate of the human creature's status and destiny, there are things other than the processes of growth, feeding, job-getting, money-making, and status-seeking to be taken into account. Love has to be reckoned with: pain has to be reckoned with: self-sacrifice as a phenomenon in others has to be noted. Why are these reminders necessary? The fact that we have to keep tacking on to our central image of man, our mental human norm, such "additional" experiences as love, suffering, and self-sacrifice, gives these experiences a peripheral status which is grotesquely out of keeping with their true significance. Yet it cannot be denied that the modern mind is such that this process of forced remembering has to be stimulated repeatedly. And not only are experiences like love, suffering, and self-surrender treated as "additional" data, experiences virtually extraneous to the human machine in its essential nature, but activities such as those which produce poetry, music, and craftsmanship are similarly categorized by implication as extra-mural to the central fabric of existence and activity which constitutes being human.

Begin a public lecture with the sentence *Man eats and drinks* and you will be accused of having uttered a platitudinous truism. Begin your lecture with the sentence *Man is an artist* or *Man is a worshipper* and you will be attended to for the moment as a man of wisdom and vision who obviously has something rather novel and striking to say. Of course your statement is a bit of an exaggeration, rather rhetorical, and consequently needs to be taken with a pinch of salt. But it is a stimulating opening. It promises well. No doubt you will soon amplify your case and drop the initial oversimplification. For surely you are the last man to pretend that being an artist or a worshipper has the same sort of connection with our essential and inescapable human lot as having breakfast or earning a salary has! We must have no extravagance, please. We must keep our heads. Nevertheless you have made a most interesting point.

A concealed preference for basic man as the walking computer constitutes a predisposition against the religious. Even those of us most firmly committed to a religious view of life feel that we have to prove our case for the religious over against an unquestionable human premiss—that of basic man the space-filling calculator who might or might not be equipped with radar devices susceptible of receiving signals from the dimension of the "other". We never seem to find ourselves in a climate of opinion which presupposes the religious premiss and is sceptical in advance of all other premisses. That is to say, we never seem to find ourselves in a climate of opinion which presupposes basic man as consciousness geared to what is other than its current functioning, and cased in an apparent but possibly illusory three-dimensional cabinet which might or might not be involved in competition for the occupancy of space alongside the other furnishings, real or illusory, of this insecure little foothold known as finitude. I do not of course press this latter premiss as a philosophical starting-point; but I argue that it is certainly no less valid than the former premiss.

The concept of man's nature which is tacitly postulated on a basis of maximal popular irrefutability in a predominantly materialistic and mechanistic age provides no ground for healthy philosophical or religious thinking. In this respect pseudo-theology has run riot. A distressing number of writers in the religious field do their work under the primary theological disqualification of having swallowed a perverted secularism's doctrine of man, hook, line, and sinker. While painfully struggling to digest this destructive diet, they set about the attempt to heal their strained throats and gullets by gargling with a disinfectant compounded of dilute Teutonic metaphysical mishmash and Freudian soda-water. It is scarcely surprising that their subsequent utterances give us a good deal of clinically useful information about the neuroses and irrationalities of the too-comfortable middle-class mid-century man, while telling us nothing at all that can shed light on the real human predicament of the men and women whose labours keep scholars and teachers and writers well-fed and warm.

Science (much of it out-of-date science, as I have shown), technology, and a "common sense" now geared to it, have trained us to a superficially rational synthesis of the data provided by our contact with the objective world at the physical level of "necessity" at which we move about without too many collisions, feed ourselves, keep ourselves comfortable and healthy, enjoy the pleasures of breeding, and prolong existence as long as possible. (May I, in parenthesis, make the point that, under each of the five heads just listed, we are in fact, in spite of our superficial rationality and system, operating with a questionable degree of efficiency and effectiveness. That is to say, we are increasingly getting in one another's way and colliding together disastrously in moving about our planet. We are feeding ourselves very inequitably, leaving a tragic proportion of our numbers to starve. We are making progress medically and surgically only to indulge in a self-inflicted cancer-of-the-lung epidemic and self-destruction by means of drugs. We are organizing, disinfecting, and—as we think—maximizing the pleasures of sexuality only at a terrific cost in broken homes, discarded lives, and sickened minds. We are lengthening life-spans often by keeping stroke-wracked minds and bodies fumbling and stumbling through days it might have been better never to have seen.

In short, in terms of movement, nourishment, health, generation, and sheer physical continuance—the processes and conditions which constitute the minimal existential recipe for basic man as now conceived—we are managing things much worse than we would like to suppose.)

Basic man, as thus imaged and noisily (if ineffectively) catered for according to the current recipe of minimal necessity, represents a twentieth-century myth which must eventually take its place among the wilder superstitions of history. Basic man eats, grows, makes money, consumes goods, contributes to the operation of the social machinery, breeds, and dies. On to basic man we try to tack, first literacy, then culture if he can take it. On to basic man we also try to tack those additional sensitivities which would transform the crude business of breeding into a varied and enjoyable venture in the manufacture of relationships and family groupings. And there are those among us who would also try to tack on to basic man an interest and concern in what is called a religious dimension—a dimension of whose validity none is sure, many are sceptical, and most are doubtful. These attempts to tack inessential, though perhaps highly desirable additional concerns on to the experience of basic man are part of a process of enrichment which will make the progress from cradle to grave more endurable, enjoyable, and worth while.

There you have it in a nutshell—the tacitly accepted though rarely articulated philosophy of our age. It is neat, economical. For basic man is such that anybody is free to come along and tack anything he likes on to it. He is encouraged by the political and cultural "establishment" to tack as much as possible on to it; to enrich it in every way possible with the maximum number and variety of enrichments from the great realms of the mind and the spirit—the arts, the sciences, the crafts, the philosophies, the religions, of knowing man. But one thing our "establishment" will not readily allow you to do, and that is to question the fundamental concept of basic man itself—and the equal right of anyone and everyone to tack whatever he likes on to it. For to question that concept may be dangerous to those delusions on which our acquisitive society is built, dangerous above all to that tidy balance of disagreements which constitutes the cement of our civilization. Thus to question this concept is generally to provoke the cry that one is being fanatical or obscurantist, idealistic or unrealistic, extravagant or rhetorical. Quite so. The question that deeply probes our smugness, our self-satisfaction, our contentment with the *status quo*, or our sense of security, will always tempt us to blanket the questioner, to hope that he did not mean what he said, to turn away and pretend that perhaps he did not say anything after all.

Nevertheless, it is a Christian duty to say, and go on saying, that basic man, as currently imaged, is a figure of myth derivative from the one mythology which the so-called de-mythologizers have not thought of de-mythologizing—the mythology of their own age.

Consider an aspect of human experience which all men face, which is a source of daily concern to them, and yet which the popular concept of the human norm not only ignores but virtually denies. I refer to the recurring pattern of minor and major disappointments which punctuate our lives. Whoever we are, of whatever social position, however rich or poor, our course through life presents us with a mixture of joys and fulfilments, disappointments and frustrations. We treat the former as analogically significant. The latter we tend to treat as flukes and freaks, mishaps and deviations from normality, peculiar to ourselves and indicative of our "bad luck". Thus, when we look back on our own past, our minds readily breed such thoughts as, "If only at that time I had . . ." or "It was a pity that just then, when . . ." which imply that a straight and naturally fruitful course was lost by unnatural and fluky deflection. But, as we grow older and become acquainted with others, listen to them (if we acquire the art of listening), and as we read and reflect on what we read, the truth dawns on us that to every man his course through life looks exactly the same in this respect.

At last you get the money you always so badly needed—and your health breaks down. At last you achieve the success long sought in a chosen field—and your wife dies. At last you gain the promotion coveted and deserved over many years—and your son is killed in a motor crash.

These are the high examples of a process which is going on all the time. Everybody's life looks thus to the man himself—an odd sequence of most unfortunate mischances marring (in some degree) a pattern of experience which would in more "normal" circumstances (without the mischances) have been an otherwise reasonably satisfactory career. In other words, we all see our lives as broken patterns. Yet we all tend to think, unless we force ourselves, as here, that in the case of others there are complete patterns, rounded careers, shaped courses from youth to age which have the grace and charm and satisfyingness of works of art.

The universality of the pattern of disappointment is quite a staggering thing to contemplate. It is closely involved with another recurring pattern which we can best characterize by the proposition, *Joys are almost always unexpected.* In big things and in little things we find that when we look for joys and successes, disappointments and failures accrue; when we look for nothing, joys and successes unexpectedly descend upon us. When the thought occurs to you that the postman might bring you something very welcome and delightful to-day, he does not call at all. When your thoughts are far away from posts and postmen, he brings you delightful news. Nothing fails so surely as the over-planned holiday, the too highly anticipated party, the excitedly awaited reunion. Nothing so surely fails to materialize as the success meticulously organized in advance. Eventually we get wise. "You mustn't look forward to it too much, or you'll be sure to be disappointed." "I always tell myself it's going to fail, and then things don't seem to turn out so badly after all." We get wise; we organize our personal defences against this thing called "luck" or "fate" or "Providence", pretend not to be looking for something when really we are looking very hard, feign a lack of interest when we are really deeply concerned, hoping that "It" can somehow be taken in. We devise little tricks. ("My dear, I never open my letters till the evening, so that I can spend all day thinking there *might* be something nice—a real break.") We systematize our defensive contrivances into superstitions and habitual eccentricities.

On the trivial level the balancing acts we perform over the abysses of disappointment are perhaps funny; but the principle discerned in things, which gives rise to our caution, is not trivial. Even in religious experience it is just when one's faith gets that extra corroboration at the rational level that something happens which assails it at the personal or emotional level. You read a book which at last washes away all your doubts about the doctrine of the Trinity, and your intellectual understanding of the faith achieves a coherence and conviction it never had before. And at the same time you find a drabness, a dryness descending upon your prayer life, and every scrap of feeling for the numinous is taken from you. Emotionally speaking, you are suddenly "dead" to the faith. Or else, perhaps a new friendship introduces you to the immediate and compelling impact of a wholly God-centred man, shedding light and warmth on everyone he meets, and soon afterwards you are afflicted by new and strange doubts as to whether the universe needs a God at all.

I claim that all this is data fundamental to the concept of "basic man" from which alone rational discussion of the human situation can begin. It is data that provides evidence of the character of "basic man" which is no less essential than the fact that man has a three-dimensional body and a tendency to consume food and drink. Man is continually being disappointed, frustrated, teased with expectations and then "let down", led up the garden path, played with on the end of a stick, lured to hope and then smacked down, probed, harried, all but taunted and tortured. (Is it the Devil who would urge me at this point to say how much more deeply in sympathy one sometimes feels with men who blaspheme God by hating him for the miseries they say he causes than those who blaspheme him by sentimentalizing him into abstract "Love"?)

One thing our objective study of the universe has surely taught us is that the things in it belong together. They fit one another. Our senses match the world in which they operate. Animals and insects serve decipherable functions in relation to their natural environment. The human brain is equipped with mechanisms for making sense of and utilizing the world's resources. Our bodies, our world, and our consciousness co-operate together and the result is the multiform, numberless experiences which we call seeing a sunset, taking a bathe, enjoying a sail, falling in love, seeing a joke, bringing up a family, singing songs, studying philosophy, admiring pictures. There seems to be some design in it all. Or at least, if design is too strong a word, there is apparently a system of relatedness and inter-relatedness by which whatever is, in this universe, belongs there and matches the rest in such a way as to contribute to some harmony or wholeness.

And yet through the course of all human lives runs this inescapable series of disappointments and frustrations, recurring experiences ceaselessly putting us consciously out of gear with the direction of things which nature and inclination urge us to expect and to hope for. If the human being is truly of a piece with the rest of things, then he must assume that the joy/disappointment and success/failure rhythm fits his rôle in some overall scheme, is designed for his personality, to call out something that no treatment less drastic than teasing and disappointing, luring and letting down, could bring into play.

As Christians, of course, we know the purpose of this rhythm that lures and sears, tempts and probes. It is to prevent the personality from feeling fully and finally and satisfyingly at home in its terrestrial environment. It achieves its purpose by a delicate balance, so that all hope in the earthly is not torn away, all confidence and aspiration lost. It works to shake our trust in the reliability of the earthly as the fitting object of the heart's dreams and the mind's ambitions, whilst yet not obliterating but preserving the assumption that good predominates and is in the long run more powerful than evil, that joy is real and in the long run more valid than suffering.

But this special knowledge of the Christian is not what I wish to press upon the reader most strongly at this point. Rather I wish to argue that any concept of man which overlooks this joy–disappointment rhythm is just as deficient as a starting-point for reflection as a concept of man would be which ignored his need for food and for drink. And in particular I wish to draw attention to the bias of current selectivism, as evidenced in popular thinking, and as commercially encouraged by high-pressure advertising, which would make of life's joys and successes a pattern analogously significant, so that they seem to evidence a norm— and thereby give the human earthly course a significance which *in fact* no thoughtful man can find in his own case—and which conversely would make of life's disappointments and failures a series of exceptions, deviations, and abnormalities, worrying as particulars, but of little theoretical weight in constructing a total picture and reason of things.

When we sit down to start an argument—with unbelievers or between ourselves, in actual discussion or in writing—we naturally seek some common ground, some universally acceptable premiss. I suggest that there are better reasons for starting with some such base as "Life is obviously some kind of test purposely planned for human beings" than for starting with some such base as "We are living solid bodies existing alongside other solid bodies, some living, some inanimate". To start with the latter axiom is no longer required of us by modern science.

And it is to start with a premiss which gives ground to the materialist in advance. The former premiss can be as surely adduced from recurring human experience, rationally weighed, as any comparable generalization. By comparison with it, the presuppositions which support the current popular, publicity-fed picture of the human situation are laden with superstition.

We end where we began. For the notion that life on this earth is some kind of test or preparation for a life beyond is in part derived from the very same "feel" of things, or, to put it more technically, is in part deduced from the identical evidence, which leads others to "read" the past and the present as a long exploratory preparation for the future. In short, the idea of inevitable progress is the secularist's version, or, if you like, the materialist's perversion, of the Christian's recognition that finitude in itself is not enough.

It all depends which way you look at things. The secularist, sensing the inadequacy of the earthly present, focuses his gaze on the earthly future, and the materialistic doctrine of progress is born. The Christian, sensing the inadequacy of the earthly present in itself, focuses his gaze on the heavenly infinite, and what happens?

Many things happen. Among them, this. The Christian is freed from servitude to the temporal on the spiritual, the moral, and the intellectual planes. He finds that the meaning, purpose, justification, and happiness towards which others reach vainly in the temporal future are in fact on offer to the present in the eternal.

As this involves acceptance of self-surrender as a spiritual principle, and of obedience as a moral principle, so too it involves acceptance of the dogmatic in the intellectual field. For in the dogmatic the eternal is framed in temporal terms.

There is no human escape from creed and dogma except by way of rebellion against God. Face to face with seeming dogma, we have the right, even the duty, to ask: "Is this the real thing, or is it spurious?" But that is an entirely different question from, "Have *we* established the truth *yet*?" Dogma is too important to be allowed to continue without examination of its credentials. But that examination is one for the whole Church extended through time, and any presupposition that the nineteen-sixties are automatically likely to be better at the job than the sixteen-sixties must be ruled out of court in advance; for that presupposition would bring back the false doctrine of progress by the back door, subtly reimposing that servitude to the temporal, that tyranny of the future, which Christian spirituality, morality, and reason alike reject.